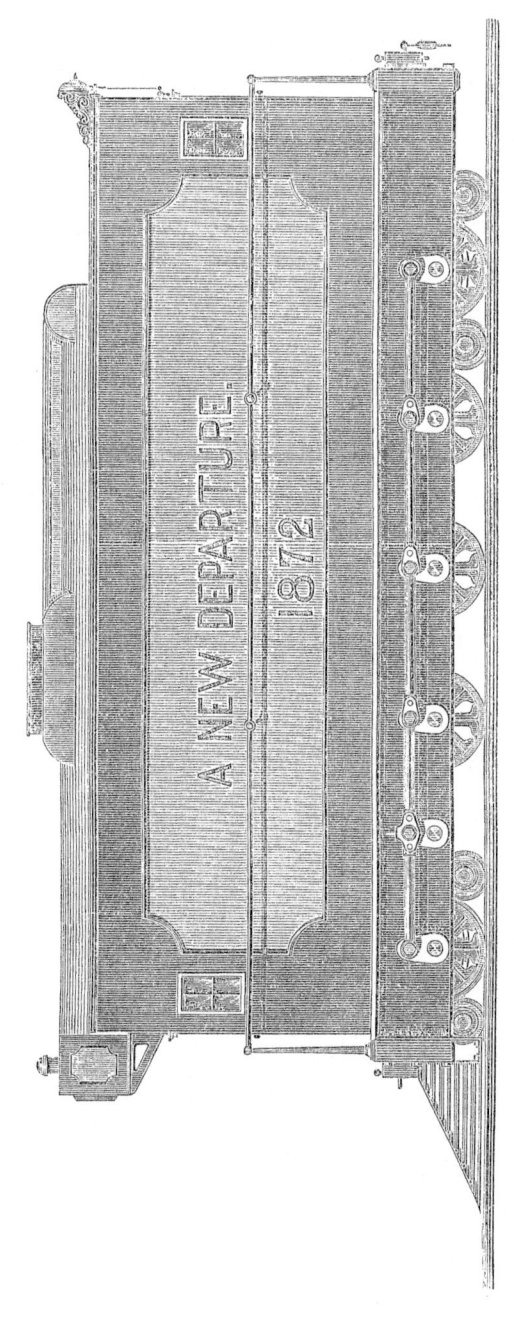

"A NEW DEPARTURE."

Design for a new Locomotive for freight. By JOSEPH HARRISON, Jr. Philadelphia, 1872.

THE
Locomotive Engine,

AND

PHILADELPHIA'S SHARE IN ITS EARLY IMPROVEMENTS.

BY

JOSEPH HARRISON, JR.

Mechanical Engineer.

REVISED EDITION WITH AN APPENDIX.

A Paper read before the members of the Franklin Institute. February 21st, 1872. First published in "The Journal of the Franklin Institute," in March and April, 1872.

PHILADELPLIA:
GEORGE GEBBIE, - - SANSOM STREET,
1872.

Entered, according to Act of Congress, in the year 1872, *by*
GEORGE GEBBIE,
In the Office of the Librarian of Congress, at Washington, D. C.

WILLIAM P. KILDARE, PRINTER.

PREFACE.

The author of this paper, wishing that Philadelphia and her engineers and mechanics, should have their deserved meed of credit in the development and in the improvement of what must be admitted to be the most important machine of modern times, has brought together in it, facts in relation to the early story of the locomotive engine in Philadelphia which, from 1820 to 1843, came under his own knowledge and supervision. He states nothing that he did not see between these years. From 1843 to the present the story is better known to all, and great as are the improvements that have since been made in the same field, they cannot be deemed so important or interesting as those of the earlier period. No controversy is invited as to when or where or by whom the first locomotive was built and started in the United States; but even in this, if Oliver Evans' claims are admitted, Philadelphia might fairly claim precedence over any other place at home or abroad. It is the permanent practical and useful results that the author insists upon, and when these are justly measured, Philadelphia may well be proud of her high position.

JOSEPH HARRISON, Jr.

RITTENHOUSE SQUARE,
Philadelphia, February 22, 1872.

TABLE OF CONTENTS.

	Page.
Allen, Horatio, Locomotives for South Carolina Railroad	23
" " Trial of first Locomotive in America	24
American Steam Carriage Company	25
Baldwin, Matthias W., First Locomotive in Philadelphia Museum	27
" " "Old Ironsides"	32
" " Locomotive of 1837	39
" " improved crank axle	40
" " opinion of the eight-wheeled in 1838	54
" " opinion of the eight-wheeled in 1845	54
" " improvements in the freight engine	59
" " Locomotive Works, Philadelphia, in 1872	59
Baltimore and Ohio Railroad, Charter of 1827	18
" " " Premium and trial of Locomotive thereon, 1831	24
Beaver Meadow Railroad, Locomotive engine for	43
" " Trial of "Samuel D. Ingham" on	45
" " " " "Hercules" on	49
"Black Hawk," Locomotive of that name	34
Brooks, James & Co., Locomotive built by	56
" " " Second Locomotive built by	57
Camden and Amboy Railroad	23
Campbell, Henry R., patented eight-wheeled engine	46
" " Trial on Philadelphia and Germantown Railroad	46
" " sale of Patent to M. Baldwin	54
" " builds six-wheeled engines	55
Child's Locomotive for Baltimore and Ohio Railroad, trial 1831	29
Columbia Railroad	31
Cooper, Peter, vertical tubular boiler	29
Costell, Stacey, experimental Locomotive, 1831	30

v

CONTENTS.

Page.
Davis, Phineas, Locomotive, 1831............................... 29
Delaware and Hudson Railroad, English Locomotive, 1829...... 24

Evans, Oliver, Petition to the Legislature of Pennsylvania...... 12
" " " " Maryland......... 13
" " secures the exclusive right to use steam carriages in Maryland, 1786............................. 13
" " makes the first useful high-pressure steam engine. 13
" " Latrobe's report against his steam carriages...... 14
" " Statement addressed to Lancaster Turnpike Co... 15
" " "Oructor Amphibolis," or amphibious digger 16
" " his prophecy as to use of steam carriages......... 17
" " comparison with English Engineers of 1829...... 18
" " "Young Millwrights' Guide".................... 19
" " Grain Elevators and improvements in milling..... 19
" " Death of.. 19
Eastwick, Andrew M., improved reversing apparatus for Locomotives................................... 43
" " " improvements in Campbell's eight-wheel engine................................. 47
" " " goes to St. Petersburgh, Russia.......... 54
Engineers and Mechanics, Philadelphia........................ 60

Fairlie Locomotive Engine..................................... 24

Galloway, Steam Boiler.. 30
Garrett & Eastwick, First Locomotive built by them............ 43
Garrett, Eastwick & Co., "Hercules," Engine.................. 47
"George Washington," Locomotive of that name............... 36
"Gowan & Marx," Locomotive of that name.................. 50
" " Peculiar construction...................... 50
" " G. N. Nicols' report on a remarkable load drawn by................................ 51
" " attracts the attention of Russian engineers Colonels Melnikoff and Krafft............ 52
" " plan of, adopted for the St. Petersburgh and Moscow Railroad......................... 52
" " Ten engines of same plan built at Lowell for Reading Railroad........................ 52

Harrison, Mr., a prominent director of the Liverpool & Manchester Railroad, recommends a premium of £550 for the best Locomotive.................................... 10

CONTENTS.

	Page.
Harrison, Joseph, Jr., foreman for Garrett & Eastwick	43
" " " partner of Philip Garrett & A. M. Eastwick,	46
" " " improvement in the eight-wheeled engine, for equalizing weight on the driving wheels, patent for	49
" " " devises a flexible truck	50
" " " improvement in connecting rod, stub ends	48
" " " goes to St. Petersburgh, Russia	52
" " " makes a contract with the Russian Government	53
" " " designs a right-angle crank boring machine,	53
Holloway, Thomas, commences to build a Locomotive	31
"Hercules," Locomotive of that name	47
" success of, on Beaver Meadow Railroad	49
"Ingham, Samuel D.," Locomotive of that name	45
Johnson, Nicholas and James, build a steam carriage to run on a common road	20
Trials of same, at Kensington, Philadelphia	20
Jenkins, Matthew C., Director of Beaver Meadow Railroad	48
" " " his confidence in the eight-wheeled Locomotive	48
Knight, Jonathan, Chief-Engineer of the Baltimore and Ohio Railroad	24
" " recommends a premium of $4000 for the best American Locomotive	25
Latrobe, B. H., report on Evans' Steam-Carriage and on Steamboats	14
Lewis, W. D., report of trial of Col. Stephen H Long's locomotive on the Newcastle and Frenchtown Railroad	25
" " recommends M. W. Baldwin for putting two English built engines on the above road	32
Liverpool and Manchester Railroad Co	9
" " " prize offered by	10
" " " locomotives entered for the prize	11
" " " trial of locomotives	11
Livingston, Chancellor, letter to Col. Stevens	6
Locomotive, the name not used in 1824	8
" "Rocket," the original engine, deposited in South Kensington Museum, London	5

CONTENTS.

	Page.
Locomotive compared with previous modes of transport	22
" early English Locomotives	9
" "Planet," first english standard	12
" first American; built by O. Evans	16
" Horatio Allen's, 1831	23
" Fairlie's	24
" "Lion." 1829	24
" first one made by Col. Stephen H. Long, 1831	25
" M. W. Baldwin's, in Philadelphia Museum, 1831	27
" reward offered for best American, by Baltimore and Ohio Railroad	24
" Phineas Davis', 1831	29
" Childs', 1831	29
" Peter Cooper's	29
" Stacy Costell's, 1831	30
" Thomas Holloway's, 1831	31
" Stephenson's, Newcastle-upon-Tyne	31
" Baldwin's "Old Ironsides," 1832	32
" " second engine	34
" Col. S. H. Long's "Black Hawk." 1833	34
" Wm. Norris' "George Washington," 1837	36
" Baldwin's, 1837	
" Garrett & Eastwick's "S. D. Ingham," 1835	43
" Eastwick's improvement in reversing the	43
" " " for equalizing weight on driving wheels of	47
" Garrett, Eastwick & Co.'s "Hercules," 1837	47
" Henry R. Campbell's first eight-wheeled, 1836	46
" J. Harrison, Jr.'s improvement on	48
" " " "	49
" Eastwick & Harrison's "Gowan and Marx," 1839	51
" " " "Beaver,"	53
" " " "Mercury," 1842	54
" M. W. Baldwin's first eight-wheeled, 1845	54
" H. R. Campbell's six-wheeled	55
" Samuel Wright's first	56
" " " second	57
" Charles and Escoll Sellers'	58
" Edward Young's improvements	58
" Leonard Phleger's "	58
" Septimus Norris' ten-wheeled	58
" possible improvements thereon	
Long, Stephen H., First Locomotive	25

CONTENTS.

Page.

Long, Stephen H., establishes the American Steam Carriage Co. 25
" " trial of his first Locomotive 25
" " his Locomotive "Black Hawk," description of, 34
" " crank axle of same.......................... 35
" " driving-wheel tires on same..................

Maryland, State of, charters first Railroad in America.......... 18
" " grant to Oliver Evans..................... 13
Museo Borbonico, ancient boiler therein....................... 4
"Mercury," Locomotive of that name, performance of.......... 55

Norris, Long &, "Black Hawk" Locomotive.................. 34
" Wm. & Co., built the "George Washington"............. 36
" William, establishes a Locomotive works in Vienna, Austria,... 38
" " Locomotive ....
" Richard, Norris Locomotive works..................... 36
" Septimus, designs a ten-wheel Locomotive 58
Nicols, G. N., Report of performance of "Gowan & Marx"...... 51
Newcastle and Frenchtown Railroad, trial of Col. Long's Locomotive thereon.. 25

"Oructor Amphibolis," of OliverEvans................. 16
"Old Ironsides," Locomotive of that name..................... 32
Oliver Evans.. 12

Philadelphia Engineers and mechanics 60
" and Reading Railroad Locomotive for,............ 50
" Germantown and Norristown Railroad. Trial of "Ironsides," thereon......................... 32
" Trial of "Black Hawk" thereon................. 34

Pardee, A., Chief-Engineer of Beaver Meadow Railroad. Confidence in eight-wheeled Locomotive....................... 48
Phleger, Leonard, makes improvements in the Locomotive....... 58

Russian engineers Melnikoff and Krafft, visit United States...... 52
contract of Harrison, Winans & Eastwick with government of... 52
Robinson, Moncure, orders Locomotive "Gowan & Marx" of Eastwick & Harrison......... 50
"Rocket," Locomotive of that name............................ 11
" preserved in South Kensington Museum, London.... 5
" wins the prize on Liverpool and Manchester Railroad. 5
Railways, early English lines................................. 7

CONTENTS.

Page.

Steam Carriage, Oliver Evans first project of.................... 12
   "   "   offer to build..................... 15
   "   "   trial of his first.................. 16
   "   "   prophecy as to future of........... 17
   "   N. & J. Johnson's............................. 20
Stephenson, George and Robert, build the Locomotive "Rocket" 11
St. Petersburgh and Moscow Railroad........................... 52

Winans, Thomas, joins A. M. Eastwick & J. Harrison, Jr., in a contract with the Russian Government...................... 52
Wright, Samuel, designs a Locomotive for James Brooks & Co... 56
   his second Locomotive....................... 57

Young, Edward, makes improvements in the Locomotive........ 58

APPENDIX.

"Lines to a Locomotive," by the Hon. Wm. D. Lewis.......... 65

"Steam Ships vs. Sailing Ships," by Joseph Harrison, Jr 66

A.—Report of Committee on Science and the Arts of The Franklin Institute, on Eastwick and Harrison's Eight-wheeled Locomotive (Reprinted from "Journal of Franklin Institute." Vol. XXIII, 1839.)....................................... 67

B.—Report of G. N. Nicols, Supt. of Philadelphia and Reading Railroad, on the performance of the Locomotive, "Gowan and Marx," February 20th, 1840. (Reprinted from "Journal of Franklin Institute." Vol. XXV, 1840.)............... 73

C.—Letter of Charles Moering, Captain of Engineers in the Austrian Army, to Eastwick and Harrison, on their Eight-wheeled Locomotive Engine, Sept. 1st, 1840. (Reprinted from "Journal of Franklin Institute." Vol. XXVI, 1840.). 76

D.—Report of G. N. Nicols, Supt. of Philadelphia and Reading Railroad, on the performance of Baldwin's geared truck Locomotive, February 12th, 1842. (Reprinted from "Journal of Franklin Institute." March, 1842................. 85

THE LOCOMOTIVE ENGINE

AND

Philadelphia's Share in its Early Improvement.

BY JOSEPH HARRISON, JR.,
MECHANICAL ENGINEER.

SOME persons care little or nothing for the past. Musty records and old things have no charm for them, and their lives seem centred in the one word, "Now." Perhaps they may be right in their abstract way of viewing the question, and they might well be pardoned for saying *cui bono*.

Others, again, omit nothing in their efforts to explore all that can be possibly reached for record or memorial, telling of the earlier days of the world on which we live, and of the doings of the inhabitants thereof. They never weary in lavishing time, trouble and expense, in following their favorite pursuit, and often are fully repaid, after long and laborious research, in the mere bringing to light of some trifling relic of may be doubtful value, or some record not worth perhaps, the time it has taken to secure it.

In the researches of the antiquary, how little however is brought out of the inner workings of the individual minds which have evolved the beautiful and the practical, in Art, in Science, and in Mechanism, even in comparatively recent days. It is the detail of their work that those interested in the subject so much desire and do not find. They would know the ways and the means, and the chain of reasoning or experiment, whereby these early workers produced the results that are left to us. And how interesting is the little that has come down to our time.

The engineer, noting the curious things in bronze and in copper, exhumed at Pompeii, and gathered together in the Museo Borbonico, at Naples, will linger near a small vessel for heating water, little more than a foot high, in which are combined nearly all the principles involved in the modern vertical steam boiler—fire-box, smoke-flue through the top, and fire-door at the side, all complete;—and strange to say, this little thing has a *water-grate*, made of small tubes crossing the fire-box at the bottom, an idea that has been patented twenty times over, in one shape or another, within the period of the history of the steam engine.

The architect, looking at the faded drawings made many centuries ago, and still serving as a guide in the completion of that epic in stone, the wonderful Cathedral on the banks of the Rhine, at Cologne, is interested not only in the beautiful forms and proportions portrayed in these now dim lines, made by the architect whose name is still preserved to us, but in noting the changes and alterations that mark their gradual approach towards perfection; showing plainly that revision and variation from the original design, was as necessary then as now, if perfection is to be achieved.

There are even still extant in record, if not in drawings, examples of Roman architecture indicating the same slow approach towards a more perfect ending, in the erection of the monuments that now excite our wonder, built to adorn the Capitol of the world more than two thousand years ago.

Knowing what we know, and seeing what we see of improvement and advancement in mechanical and engineering science and art all around us, how interesting it is to look at the first condensing steam engine made by James Watt, and the little locomotive "Rocket," of George and Robert Stephenson, both so carefully preserved in the South Kensington Museum, in London.

The history of a most remarkable machine, now so necessary in our daily wants, had its really useful commencement but forty years ago, and yet much that is exceedingly interesting in the detail of its early introduction and improvement is unknown to this generation, or has already become tradition,— and before many years are passed all those who labored at its beginning, and who only can tell the story of its early progress towards its present perfection from their personal knowledge, will have passed away.

To prevent this loss in part, an effort will be

made in the following pages, and without going too much into technical detail, to bring together some facts in connection with the early and very important work of Philadelphia Mechanics and Engineers in the the origination, and in the development of the improvements in the LOCOMOTIVE ENGINE. No controversy will be invited as to when or where or by whom the first locomotive was built and started in the United States; but even in this, if Oliver Evans' claims are admitted, Philadelphia might fairly claim precedence over any other place at home or abroad. It is the practical and the permanent useful results that will be insisted upon only, and when these are justly measured, Philadelphia may well be proud of her high position.

The following letter from Chancellor LIVINGSTONE to Col. STEVENS, of Hoboken, fairly represents the public opinion of that time, and is most interesting as a contribution to the history of railroads. It is dated March 2, 1811, and is written from Albany.

"I had before read of your very ingenious proposition as to railway communication. I fear, however, on mature reflection, that they will be liable to serious objections, and ultimately prove more expensive than a canal. They must be double, so as to prevent the danger of two such heavy bodies meeting. The wall on which they are to be placed must be at least four feet below the surface to avoid frost, and three feet above to avoid snow, and must be clasped with iron, and even then would hardly sustain so heavy a weight as you propose moving at the rate of four miles (!) an hour on wheels. As to wood, it would not last a week. They must be covered with iron, and that, too, very thick and strong. The means of stopping these heavy carriages without a great shock, and of preventing them from running on each other, for there would be many running on the road at once—would be very difficult. In case of accidental stops, or necessary stops to take wood and water, &c., many accidents would happen. The carriage of condensing water would be very troublesome. Upon the whole, I fear the expense would be much greater than that of canals, without being so convenient."

In the opening part of an article printed in a supplement to the Encyclopædia Brittanica, 1824, may be found the following: "RAILWAYS.—A species of road or carriage way, in which the track of the carriage wheels being laid with bars or rails of wood, stone or metal, the carriage is more easily drawn over this smooth surface than over an ordinary road." And further, in the same article, after alluding to the early history of railways in Great Britain, and touching on the chief lines then in use, the article continues: "From these accounts of the chief railways in England and Wales, it will appear that this species of inland carriage is principally applicable where trade is considerable, and the length of the conveyance short, and is chiefly useful in transporting the mineral products of the kingdom from the mines to the nearest land or water communication, whether sea, river or canal. Attempts have been made to bring it into more general use, but without success, and it is only in particular circumstances that navigation, with the aid of locks or inclined planes to surmount the elevations, will not present a more convenient medium for an extended trade.

"South Wales, however, presents an example where the trade being great, and also chiefly descending, the country rugged, and the supply of water scant, railways have been adopted with complete success, and have been found, in some cases at least, equal to canals in point of economy and dispatch." After further discussing the topic, the conclusion of the article is as follows: "On some of the railways near Newcastle, the wagons are drawn by a steam engine placed on a wagon by itself, the wheels of which are driven by the engine, and, acting on a rack laid along the railway, impel forward the engine and the attached wagons. In some cases, the wheels of the wagon operate without rack-work, by the mere friction between them and the rail. The steam engines employed for this purpose are of the high-pressure kind, these requiring no condensing apparatus."

"But this application of steam has not yet arrived at such perfection as to have brought it into general use."

When it is considered that but a generation and a half has passed since its publication, the above reads strangely in the light of our present knowledge and experience. It is noteworthy, too, that in the article from which the above extracts have been taken, there is not one word in relation to the transportation of passengers by railroad, nor is the name of "Locomotive," since become so distinguished, once used.

During the five years following the year 1824, little was done towards the improvement of the motive power for working the railroads of Great Britain, the only country in which they were used. In 1829, when the Liverpool and Manchester Railroad (the pioneer of a new system which has since attained such tremendous proportions) was well advanced towards completion, the locomotive was so unimportant an agent, that it was not even then easy to decide the question of motive power for working that important line. The locomotive had its friends in the Stephensons, father and son, in Hackworth, Braithwaite and Erickson, Trevethick and others. A plan for placing fixed steam engines at intervals along the line to draw the trains by endless ropes running over pulleys, had its supporters. Horses were looked to as a safe means to fall back upon when all else should fail. A machine to use horse power was even thought of, and was afterwards built, in which the propelling horses were carried on the carriage that was to be used for drawing the train.

During the year 1828 it became imperative, on the part of the Directors of the Liverpool and Manchester Railway, to decide in some way the question of motive power, and in that year a deputation of this body "was appointed to visit the railways of Northumberland and Durham, where the different varieties of motive power were most extensively practiced." This deputation returned from this mission without coming to any conclusion as to which class of motive power would most conduce to their interests. They *did*, however, decide "that horse-power would be inapplicable for the great traffic that was anticipated upon the new line."

By this decision the question was narrowed down to the locomotive engine (then gradually becoming the favorite) and the fixed engine. This latter device was known to be clumsy in its management, and difficult to manage where a large traffic was to be carried on, or where it was of primary importance that greatly increased speed must be aimed at. Little scope, therefore, was left in the fixed engine system for improvement tending to meet these essentials, and little could be expected.

At this point in this most important controversy, it was suggested that the surest way to bring out the merits of the locomotive system, was to excite competition on the part of its advocates, by the offer of a premium or reward for the best locomotive engine. In the spring of 1829, and in accordance with this idea, first enunciated by Mr. Harrison, a member of the Board, it was decided by the Directors of the Liverpool and Manchester Railway, to make this premium £500, to be contended for under conditions to be fixed by the Company.

The very important conclusions which soon resulted from the competition induced by the above offer, in the rapid improvement of the locomotive engine, formed a new era, not only in *their* history, but in the importance of railways generally. The conditions upon which the premium was offered was in part, as follows:

"RAILWAY OFFICE, LIVERPOOL,
25*th of April*, 1829.

"STIPULATIONS AND CONDITIONS

On which the Directors of the Liverpool and Manchester Railway offer a premium of £500, for the most improved locomotive engine.

"1st. The said engine must 'effectually consume its own smoke,' according to Railway Act. 7th Geo. IV.

" 2nd. The engine, if it weighs six tons, must be capable of drawing after it, day by day, on a well constructed railway, on a level plane, a train of carriages of a gross weight of *twenty tons*, including the tender and water tank, at the rate of *ten miles* per hour, with a pressure of steam on the boiler of *fifty pounds* to the square inch

"8th. The price of the engine that may be accepted is not to exceed £550, delivered on the railway; and any engine not approved is to be taken back by the owner."

The following engines were entered for the prize:

    The "Novelty," by Braithwaite and Erickson.
    " "Rocket," by Robert Stephenson.
    " "Sans Pareil." by Timothy Hackworth.
    " "Perseverance," by Mr. Burstall.

All these engines had distinct principles in their construction, the most important of which being in the plan, and in the steam generating properties of the boilers.

After a fair test of all the locomotives competing in accordance with the regulations fixed, the prize was easily won by the "Rocket," built by George and Robert Stephenson; this engine having fulfilled, in some respects, more than all the requirements of the trial.

It is remarkable that the "Rocket," in all or nearly all of the general essentials that go toward making the locomotive what it is, was as complete as the engine of our day. Its weight was but 3 tons, 1 cwt. From the success achieved by the "Rocket" at Liverpool, the locomotive engine took the place it now fills so perfectly, as the great motor for land transportation.

The type of locomotive established by the success of the "Rocket" became in its immediate successor the "Planet," the then standard in England, and the Directors of the Liverpool and Manchester Railway lost no time in stocking their railway with engines mainly after this model, although some English engineers seemed still to have had doubts as to the great value of this new revelation in steam power that had been born into the world.

With this preliminary, it is now the purpose of this paper to tell the early history of the locomotive in Philadelphia, and to show how great a share the minds and hands of our engineers and mechanics have had in the improvement and development of (without doubt) the most important agent of this or any other age. In telling this completely, it will be necessary to take a retrospect and go back to the year 1786.

In that year, Oliver Evans, a man who deserves at this day all honor at our hands, as one of Philadelphia's noblest sons, "petitioned the Legislature of Pennsylvania for the exclusive right to use his improvements in flouring mills and steam carriages in his native State. In the following year he presented the same petition to the Legislature of Maryland. In the former case he was only successful so far as to obtain the privilege for the mill improvements, his representations respecting steam carriages savoring too much of insanity to deserve notice."

"He was more fortunate in Maryland, for although the steam project was laughed at, yet one of his friends a member, very judiciously observed that the grant could injure no one, for he did not think that any man in the world had ever thought of such a thing before. He therefore wished the encouragement might be afforded, as there was a prospect of its producing something useful." The exclusive privilege was granted, and after this Mr. Evans considered himself bound in honor to the State of Maryland, to produce a steam carriage as soon as his means would permit him.

To Oliver Evans must be awarded the credit of having built and put in operation the first practically useful high-pressure steam engine, using steam at 100 pounds pressure to the square inch, or more, and dispensing with the complicated condensing apparatus of Watt The high-pressure engine of Evans had advantages for us in its greater simplicity and cheapness, and ever since his day it has continued the standard steam engine for land purposes in this country.

English writers have tried to detract from the fame of Oliver Evans, but it is well known that early in his engineering life he sent drawings and specifications of his engines, &c., to England by the hands of Mr. Joseph Stacey Sampson, of Boston. It is well known also, that these drawings, &c., were shown to and copied by engineers in England, and from this period dates the introduction into Europe of the first really useful high-pressure steam engine, now so generally applied to locomotive and other purposes.

Basing his hopes of success on the use of the high-pressure engine in his steam carriage, Oliver Evans, notwithstanding the opposition and even the derision of his best friends, and of almost every one, made earnest efforts in the beginning of this century to carry out his design for building his favorite machine, but without success. He had a good friend in Mr. Robert Patterson, then Professor of Mathematics in the University of Pennsylvania, who recommended the plan as highly worthy of notice, and who wished to see it tried. Evans' plans were shown to Mr. B. H. Latrobe, a scientific gentleman of great eminence in his day, who publicly pronounced them chimerical, and who attempted to demonstrate their absurdity in his report to the American Philosophical Society on "*Steam Engines*," in which he also undertook to show the impossibility of making steamboats useful.

In Mr. Latrobe's report, Mr. Evans was said to be seized with the "*steam mania*," which was no doubt most true. To the credit of our then and now most learned Society, the portion of Mr. Latrobe's report which reflected so harshly upon Mr. Evans was rejected, the members conceiving that they had no right to set up their opinions as an obstacle in the way of an effort towards improvements that might prove valuable for transport on land. The Society did, however, admit in the report the strictures on steamboats.

Oliver Evans never succeeded in constructing a steam carriage such as he had contemplated. It was commenced, and unaided he spent much time and money in fruitless efforts to complete it. Finding himself likely to be impoverished if he persisted in the scheme, he finally abandoned it, and devoted his time thereafter to the manufacture of his high-pressure steam engine and his improved milling machinery. Previously however, to the final abandonment of his favorite project, Oliver Evans, on the 25th of September, 1804, submitted to the Lancaster Turnpike Company a statement of the cost of and probable profits of a steam-carriage to carry *one hundred* barrels of flour *fifty* miles in twenty-four hours, tending to show also that one such carriage would make more net profit on a good turnpike road than ten wagons drawn by five horses each.

He offered to build a steam carriage at a very low price. Evans' statement to the turnpike Company closed as follows: "It is too much for an individual to put in operation every improvement which he may invent. I have no doubt but that my engines will propel boats against the currents of the Mississippi, and wagons on turnpike roads with great profit. I now call upon those whose interest it is, to carry this invention into effect."

Oliver Evans, in the early part of 1804, came nearest to realizing his favorite idea, in obtaining an order from the Board of Health of Philadelphia to construct at his foundry (a mile and a half from the water) a dredging machine for cleaning docks, the first one ever contrived for dredging by steam, now so common.

To this machine Evans gave the name of "Oructor Amphibolis," or Amphibious Digger, and he determined, when it was completed, to propel it from his work shop to the Schuylkill River, which was successfully done, to the astonishment of a crowd of people gathered together to see it fail. When launched, a paddle-wheel, previously arranged, was put in motion at the stern, and again it was propelled by steam to the Delaware, leaving all vessels half-way behind in the trip, the wind being ahead.

This result Evans hoped would have settled the minds of doubters as to the value of steam as a *motor* on land and water. But his attempt at moving so great a weight on land was ridiculed, no allowance being made by the *hinderers* of that day for the disproportion of power to load,—rudeness in applying the force of steam for its propulsion, or for the ill form of the boat. A rude cut of the "Oructor Amphibolis" is still extant, which shows a common scow, mounted on four wooden wheels, with power applied to the whole number of the wheels by the use of leathern belts.

Evans, after this experiment, willing to meet the question in any way, silenced the *carpers* around him by offering a wager, that for $3,000 he would make a steam carriage that would run on a level road as swift

Oliver Evans' "Oructor Amphibolis," or Amphibious Digger.
THE FIRST AMERICAN LOCOMOTIVE.—1804.

as the fastest horse they could produce. His bet met with no takers.

This movement by steam power of Oliver Evans' dredging machine on land was, without any doubt, the first application of steam to a carriage in America, and in fact the first locomotive engine. It was a more important experiment than any that had preceded it, anywhere in the same direction.

Oliver Evans' conceptions respecting the power of steam, many of them practically exemplified by him, reflects great credit on his sagacity as an engineer, and many of his predictions in regard to its great value, particularly for land transport, may well be termed prophetic.

In the early part of this century he publicly stated that "The time will come when people will travel in stages moved by steam engines from city to city, almost as fast as birds fly,—fifteen or twenty miles an hour. Passing through the air with such velocity, changing the scene in such rapid succession, will be the most exhiliarating exercise." "*A steam carriage will set out from Washington in the morning,—the passengers will breakfast in Baltimore,—dine in Philadelphia, and sup in New York the same day.*" "To accomplish this, two sets of railways will be required, laid so nearly level as not to deviate more than two degrees from a horizontal line,—made of wood or iron, or smooth paths of broken stone or gravel, with a rail to guide the carriages, so that they may pass each other in different directions, and travel by night as well as day."

Much stress is laid upon these early efforts of Oliver Evans towards the introduction of steam for land and water transportation, and much space has been given here to set them forth. With no light to guide him (for it is fair to suppose that he knew nothing of the little that had been done up to his day in Europe), how his trumpet-tones ring out in the words above quoted, compared with the "uncertain sound" made by the English engineers in 1829. *They*, with a quarter of a century or more of later experience, during which period much had been done to improve and develope the locomotive engine, then no new thing, nor was it barren of useful practical results, hesitated and doubted in their course. *He*, with no misgivings as to the future, and with no dimmed vision, saw with prophetic eyes all that we now see. To *him* the present picture, in all its grandeur and importance, glowed in broad sunlight. In the history of these efforts of Oliver Evans it is noteworthy, and most creditable to our sister State of Maryland, that that Commonwealth extended to him the first public encouragement in his steam carriage project.

Again our enterprising neighbor was first in the field, since become so important, for we find that in March, 1827, the State of Maryland chartered the first railway company in America, and in 1828 her citizens commenced the construction of the Baltimore and Ohio Railway, aiming to cross the Alleghenies; certainly the greatest railway scheme that had been thought of up to that date, and now, in its completed

THE LOCOMOTIVE ENGINE. 19

state, a triumph of railway engineering. To this first effort to make a great railway in the United States, and its influence upon the history of the locomotive in Philadelphia, reference will be made hereafter.

Oliver Evans died in 1819, and his plans for a steam carriage died with him, and although he produced nothing practically useful in the great idea of his life, he has left behind him an enduring monument in his grain and flour machinery.

[NOTE. The improvements of Oliver Evans in grinding flour, as described in his "Young Millwrights' Guide," (a standard authority at this day on the subject of milling), changed the whole system of handling grain and its products. The principles and, in many respects, the arrangements in detail of the great grain elevators used so extensively at the present hour, came originally from the teeming brain of Evans. In the first edition of the Young Millwrights' Guide, published eighty years ago, an engraving may be seen of an elevator unloading a vessel at the river side, and conveying the grain to an upper granary on the wharf, just as it is done to-day. It is painful to read Evans' own story of his struggles against the prejudiced and doubting men of his time, in his efforts to introduce his improved milling machinery. Those who were ultimately most benefited by his inventions were his most persistent opponents. But he triumphed at last in this, although failing to get his steam carriage into use.]

The materials for the history of the next attempt at making a steam carriage in Philadelphia, eight or nine years after the death of Oliver Evans, are not very full. At this period a steam carriage to run on a common road was projected by some parties in our city whose names cannot now be easily reached. This steam carriage was built at the small engineering establishment of Nicholas and James Johnson, then doing business in Penn Street, in the old district of Kensington, just above Cohocksink Creek.

An eye witness of its construction, and who saw it running under steam on several of its trials, describes it as an oddly arranged and rudely constructed machine. It is believed to have had but a single cylinder, set horizontally, with connecting-rod attachment to a single crank at the middle of the driving axle. Its two driving wheels were made of wood, the same as an ordinary road wagon, and were of large diameter, certainly not less than eight feet. It had two smaller wheels in front, arranged in the usual manner of a road wagon, for guiding the movement of the machine. It had an upright boiler hung on behind, shaped like a huge bottle, the smoke-pipe coming out through the centre at the top, formed the neck of the bottle. Its safety valve was held down by a weight and lever, and it was somewhat amusing to see the *puff, puff, puff*, of the safety valve as the machine jolted over the rough street. This was before the days of spring balances for holding down the safety valves of locomotives.

On its trials, made on the unpaved streets of the neighborhood in which it was built, this steam carriage showed an evident lack of boiler as well as cylinder power. It would, however, run continuously for some time and surmount considerable elevations in the roads. It was sometimes a little unmanageable in the steering apparatus, and on one of its trials, in running over the High bridge and turning up Brown Street, its course could not be changed quick enough, and before it could be stopped, it had mounted the curbstone, smashed the awning posts, and had made a demonstration against the bulk window of a house at the south-west corner of Brown and Oak Streets.

After this mishap it was not seen on the streets again, nor is it known what ultimately became of it. This last effort may be classed in some respects no doubt, with what Oliver Evans promised in his mind to carry out, and it is very evident that up to its time no great amount of knowledge, or of practical or theoretical skill, had been brought to bear upon the construction of locomotives in Philadelphia. No books were as yet published in America describing the locomotive, or telling what had been done in land transport by steam in Europe. The trials on the Liverpool and Manchester railway in 1829 had not been made, and a better result could have hardly been expected than this recorded above.

With the wonderful success of the "Rocket" in October, 1829, the attention of our engineers and capitalists was strongly turned towards this new revelation in land transport, that had so suddenly flashed upon the world. It was a matter of the greatest importance to us, with our rich lands everywhere teeming with produce, the producers meanwhile crying aloud for better means to get their harvests to market, and for getting our people too, more speedily from point to point, that we should know more of this new thing, and if it fulfilled its promise, to get the advantage of it as soon as possible.

It is true that the river, the canal, and the turnpike road had done good service in the past; but they did not keep pace with the growing wants of the country. The river, Nature's own free highway, is, when navigable, often hindered by flood and frost, by currents and by drought, nor does it run everywhere, or always where it would best conduce to man's use and benefit. The slow, plodding canal did its work cheaply, and with nothing better, it must have continued the favorite means for inland trade. But canals are only possible where water can be had in abundance to keep them full, and with winter's cold to interrupt their movement, they are practically useless for half the year. Their capacity at best, is limited too, in many ways. The turnpike road, most useful in its place, had a very narrow limit of usefulness, when the means to do the the carrying trade of a continent were to be attained. Man's restless nature longed for, and demanded something better than the river, the canal, or the turnpike road, and this had been found in the RAILROAD and the LOCOMOTIVE. It did not take long, therefore, to come to a decision that railways *must* be built, and the locomotive brought into use, and that speedily.

It has been seen that Maryland took the lead, and she had her great road well under way before other States looked the question fairly in the face. South Carolina followed the lead of Maryland, and granted a charter at an early period to the South Carolina Railway, intending to cross the whole breadth of the State, and ultimately aiming to reach the far west.

Signs of railway movement were seen in Pennsylvania, Delaware and New Jersey, and in New York and New England. The Columbia railroad (a State work) was projected in Pennsylvania at this time, and the Philadelphia, Germantown and Norristown Railroad was begun in Philadelphia. New Jersey had chartered and commenced her road from Camden to Amboy, and little Delaware, ahead of all the States north and east of her, had two miles of the Newcastle and Frenchtown Railroad ready for use on the 4th of July, 1831.

The South Carolina Railroad was amongst the first to encourage the manufacture of American locomotives, and Mr. Horatio Allen, a gentleman honored still as a good citizen, and as one of the first engineers in the country, designed and had built, in 1830 and '31, at the West Point foundry in New York, the first locomotives, it is believed that were ever ordered and made in the United States for regular railroad traffic.

Other engines, subsequently built in New York after designs by Mr. Allen, did good service on the South Carolina Railroad, and it is curious to note that, in these later engines, was embodied every valuable point of the "Fairlie" engine, now making so much noise in England. These points being the use of a vibrating truck at both ends with cylinders thereon, fire-box in the middle, with flues from fire-box to each end of the boiler, double smoke-box and double chimney, with fire-door at the side of fire-box, flexible steam and exhaust pipe, &c.

[NOTE. The first locomotive ever run on a railroad in America was undoubtedly the "Lion," one of two engines built at Stourbridge, in England, under the direction of Mr. Horatio Allen, and imported into this country in the autumn of 1829, for the Delaware and Hudson Railroad in the State of New York. Mr. Allen, in describing its first movement, says that he was the only person upon the engine at the time, and he (living still) made the first trip by steam on an American railroad. The "Lion," built before the "Rocket," had vertical cylinders, arranged somewhat after the manner of the old style of Killingworth or Stockton and Darlington engines, with four driving wheels all connected. The boiler of this engine approached closely to the locomotive boiler of the present day, in having a fire-box with five flues leading to the smoke-box, this latter feature being, in fact, the first step towards the present multi-tubular boiler.]

The Directors of the Baltimore and Ohio Railroad in January, 1831, by advice of Mr. Jonathan Knight, of Pennsylvania, still taking the lead in the railroad movement, and with the desire to encourage

American skill, adopted the same plan that had been so successfully carried out at Liverpool in 1829, and offered a premium of $4,000 for the best American locomotive.

At this period in this history, more mind and more practical knowledge had been brought out in Philadelphia, aiming towards the improvement of the locomotive engine. In March, 1830, Col. Stephen H. Long, of the United States Topographical Engineers, a gentleman of high scientific culture, and noted for his originality, obtained a charter from the State of Pennsylvania, incorporating the "American Steam Carriage Company," and soon thereafter commenced the construction of a locomotive in Philadelphia. This engine was designed somewhat after the then recently improved locomotives made in England, but had several original points.

This first engine of Col. Long was placed, when finished, upon the Newcastle and Frenchtown Railroad, and the Hon. Wm. D. Lewis has furnished the following account of its trial at various times on that road, with which he at that period was connected in an official capacity.

Col. Long's Locomotive.

"On the 4th of July, 1831, two miles of the rails being laid on the Newcastle and Frenchtown Railroad, Col. Long made trial on it of his locomotive, which weighed about $3\frac{1}{2}$ tons. The first effort was not a success, the failure being attributed to lack of capacity to furnish a sufficient supply of steam. It would go well enough for a while, but the steam could not be kept up. The next day the Colonel had better luck; his engine then going to the end of our rails and back, drawing two passenger cars packed with people, (say 70 or 80,) with apparent ease, and it had fifty pounds of steam at the end of the experiment.

"The Colonel, however, was not satisfied with it, and the machine was brought to Philadelphia again, and a new boiler was constructed for it at Rush & Muhlenburgh's works at Bush Hill. This engine was again taken to Newcastle and tried upon the road but it again failed. It would go very well for a time, but on the 31st of October, 1831, a pipe was burst and it became disabled. This being repaired, two days thereafter another trial was made, but with equal want of success, which was ascribed to lack of power as well as of specific gravity. Alone, this engine went very well, and rapidly, say at the rate of 25 miles an hour, but it would not draw a satisfactory burden.

"Soon after the above date, Col. Long removed his engine from the road, and I do not know what became of it afterwards." Mr. Lewis adds, "The above memoranda I now enclose of the trials of Col. Long's locomotive in 1831, are made from a book in which all the facts I give you were set down contemporaneously with their occurrence." This unsuccessful attempt of Col. Long was, up to its date, much the most important movement that had yet been made in Philadelphia towards the improvement of the locomotive, and as such it deserves special notice. It was furthermore not without its value in inducing him thereafter to pursue the subject to much better results. Had Col. Long more faithfully copied the English engine of his day, he would have had better success in his first effort; but he, as with all our Philadelphia engineers and mechanics at that time, and in the succeeding years, aimed at making an American locomotive.

Whilst Col. Long was engaged in the construction of his engine, the late Matthias W. Baldwin, a name that has since become so famous in the history of the improvements, and in the manufacture of the locomotive in Philadelphia, was engaged in making a model locomotive for the Philadelphia Museum. In this work Mr. Baldwin was assisted by that highly eminent practical mechanic and engineer, the late Franklin Peale, then Manager of the Museum

To gratify the curiosity of the public to know more of this new thing, this little engine was placed upon a track laid around the rooms of the Museum, in what was then the Arcade, in Chestnut Street, above Sixth, and where it was first put in operation on April 25th, 1831, It made the circuit of the Museum rooms many times during the day and evening, for several months, drawing behind it two miniature passenger cars, with seats in each for four persons but often carrying twice that number, in a manner highly gratifying to the public, who attended in crowds to witness for the first time in this city and state, the effect of steam in railroad transportation. This little engine was perhaps the first made expressly to draw passengers, that had ever been placed on a railroad in America.

[Note. In rendering a just meed of credit to all who aided in the early development of the Locomotive in Philadelphia, it is not out of place here to introduce the following extract from an obituary notice of Franklin Peale, read before the American Philosophical Society at a meeting on December 16th, 1870, by his friend Robert Patterson, a grandson of Robert Patterson, who had been Oliver Evans' firm friend in the latter's efforts in the last century to introduce a steam carriage. "It was while engaged at the Museum that Mr. Peale placed there a miniature locomotive, the first seen in this country, and manufactured by his friend, M. W. Baldwin, on a plan agreed upon between Mr. Peale and his friend. It was put in operation on a track, making the circuit of the Arcade, in which the Museum then was, drawing two miniature cars with seats for four passengers. The valuable aid of Mr. Peale was afterwards given to Mr. Baldwin in the construction of the locomotive for the Philadelphia and Germantown Railroad, built in 1832, the success of which led to the establishment of Mr. Baldwin in the great business of his life."]

With the knowledge of the success that had been achieved in England, the desire to *know* more of, and the necessity to *have* as speedily as possible, this new power, soon became a paramount question in the Middle, Northern, Southern and Eastern States of the Union.

The reward of $4000 offered for the best American Locomotive by the Directors of the Baltimore and Ohio Railroad, brought out many competitors, and in after years several very curious specimens of locomotive engineering might be seen in one of the shops of this road. An eye-witness of these efforts in 1834, describes one which sported two walking beams, precisely like the river steamers of the present day. Mr. Phineas Davis, of York, Pennsylvania, bore off the prize offered by the Baltimore and Ohio Railroad, and his engine was the only one that survived the trial. With the Peter Cooper upright tubular boiler adapted thereto, this locomotive of Mr. Davis became for several years the type of engine for the road upon which it won its fame, and to this day some of these Grasshopper or Crab engines, as they are sometimes called, may be seen doing good service at the Camden Street Station, in Baltimore.*

Philadelphia mechanics, following the lead of their predecessors in the same field, entered with zeal into the Baltimore contest. An engine was built by a Mr. Childs, who had invented a rotary

*Previous to the competition on the Baltimore Railroad, Mr. Peter Cooper, the well known New York Philanthropist of the present day, sent to Baltimore, a small engine, not larger than an ordinary hand-car. This little locomotive had an upright tubular boiler, (no doubt the first of its kind,) which developed such good steam making qualities, as to induce Mr. Phineas Davis to purchase the Cooper patent right, and boilers of this kind were used by Mr. Davis in the locomotives built by him, subsequent to the competitive trial on the Baltimore and Ohio Railroad.

engine which in a small model promised good results, and an engine of about fifty horse-power on this rotary plan was built and sent to Baltimore for trial. A record of its performance cannot now be easily reached, but it is known that it was never heard of as a practically useful engine after this time.

The second locomotive built in Philadelphia, to compete at Baltimore, was designed by Mr. Stacey Costell, a man of great originality as a mechanic, and the inventor of a novelty in the shape of a vibrating cylinder steam engine, that had some reputation in its day, and has come down to our time exactly, in the little engine now sold in the toy shops for a dollar.

The Costell locomotive had four connected driving wheels, of about thirty-six inches in diameter, with two six-inch cylinders of twelve-inch stroke. The cylinders were attached to right-angled cranks on the ends of a counter shaft, from which shaft spur gearing connected with one of the axles. The boiler was of the Cornish type, with fire inside of an internal straight flue. Behind the bridge wall of this boiler, and inside the flue, water tubes, were placed at intervals, crossing each other after the manner of the English Galloway boiler of the present day. The peculiar arrangement of this engine made it possible to use a very simple and efficient mode of reversement by the use of a disc between the steam pipe and the cylinders, arranged with certain openings, which changed the direction of the steam and exhaust by the movement of this disc against a face on the steam pipe near the cylinder, something after the manner of a two-way cock.

It is not known whether this locomotive of Costell's went to Baltimore or not. It is known, however, to have been tried on the Columbia road in 1833 or 1834, but its success was not very striking, and it was subsequently broken up. The boiler of the Costell locomotive had very good steam-making qualities. It was used for a long time as a stationary engine boiler.

The third engine begun in Philadelphia for the Baltimore trial in 1831, was after a design of Mr. Thos. Holloway, an engineer of some reputation forty years ago as a builder of river steamboat engines. This engine was put in hand, but was never completed.

Something was gained even by the failures that are here related, and these early self-reliant efforts show with what tenacity Philadelphia engineers clung to the idea of building an original locomotive, and it will be seen hereafter that a type of locomotive essentially American was ultimately the result.

Whilst these movements towards the improvement of the locomotive were going on amongst us, the desire to have the railroad in every section of the country became more and more fully confirmed. The railway from Newcastle to Frenchtown, sixteen miles in length, was finished in the winter of 1831 and 1832, and two locomotives built by Robert Stephenson at Newcastle-upon-Tyne, were imported to be run upon this line, which made then an important link in the chain of passenger travel between New York and Washington. In this case, as in several others in the early history of the railroad in the United States, this new element came in as an adjunct mainly of the river steamboats, and was considered most useful in superseding the old stage coach in connecting river to river, and bay to bay.

That the railway would supersede the steamboat for passenger travel, and the canal for heavy transport, was not dreamed of in the early day of the new power.

When the English locomotives were landed at Newcastle, Delaware, it became necessary to select a skilled mechanic to put them together as speedily as possible. Through the agency of Mr. Wm. D. Lewis, a most active Director of the Newcastle and Frenchtown Railroad Company, this task was assigned to Matthias W. Baldwin. These engines were of the most improved English type, and were greatly superior in design and workmanship, to any that had then been seen in this country. In putting these engines together, Mr. Baldwin had all the advantage of handling their parts and studying their proportions, and in making drawings therefrom. This proved of great service to him when he received an order, in the spring of 1832, to build a locomotive for the Philadelphia, Germantown and Norristown Railroad. This engine, called, when finished, the "Old Ironsides," was placed upon the above road in November, 1832, and proved a decided success. Mr. Franklin Peale, in an obituary notice of M. W. Baldwin, writes, "that the experiments made with the 'Ironsides' were eminently successful, realizing the sensation of a flight through the air of fifty or sixty miles an hour." The "Old Ironsides," in its general arrangement, was a pretty close copy of the English engines on the Newcastle and Frenchtown Railroad, but with changes that were real improvements. The reversing gear was a novelty in the locomotive, although the same mode had been long used for steam ferry boats on the Delaware. This arrangement consisted of a single excentric with a double latch excentric rod, gearing alternately on pins on the upper and lower ends of the arms of a rock shaft. This mode of reversing was used in the Baldwin locomotives for many years after the "Old Ironsides" was built.

"Old Ironsides," 1832.

It is creditable to Mr. Baldwin as an engineer that the "Old Ironsides" was the first and last of his imitations of the English locomotives. He, following the bent of all the Philadelphia engineers and mechanics that had entered the field, aimed too, at making an American locomotive, and his second engine, and those succeeding it, were entirely different in design from the "Old Ironsides."

Following the success of this first locomotive, other orders soon flowed in upon Mr. Baldwin, and on these later engines many valuable improvements were introduced, of which mention will be made hereafter. Col. Stephen H. Long, nothing daunted or discouraged by the unsuccessful results of his first engine in 1831, renewed his efforts, and under the firm of Long & Norris, the successors of the American Steam Carriage Company, commenced building a locomotive in 1832, subsequently called the "Black Hawk." This engine when finished, was run for some time on the Philadelphia and Germantown Railroad, and did good service in the summer of 1833, in competition with Baldwin's "Ironsides." The "Black Hawk" burnt anthracite coal with some success, using the natural draft only, which was increased, for the first time, in a locomotive by the use of a very high chimney, arranged to lower from an altitude of at least twenty feet from the rails, to a height which enabled it to go under the bridges crossing the railroad. In all of Col. Long's experiments he seems to have discarded the steam jet, or exhaust, for exciting the fire. The "Black Hawk" had several striking peculiarities beside the one just mentioned. The boiler, a very good and a very safe one, was unlike any that had preceded it, in having the fire-box arranged without a roof, being merely formed of water sides, and in being made in a detached piece from the waist or cylindrical part. The cylinder portion of the boiler consisted of two cylinders, about twenty inches in diameter, and these lying close together, were bolted to the rear water side, and thus covered the open top, and their lower half-diameters thereby became the roof of the fire-box. A notch was cut half way through these two cylinders on their lower half-diameters about midway of the length of the fire-box, directly over the fire, and from these notches flues of about two inches diameter passed through the water space of each cylinder portion of the boiler to the smoke-box. These flues were about seven feet in length. Besides passing through the flues, the fire passed also under the lower halves of the cylinder portions of the boiler, a double sheet iron casing, filled between with clay, forming the lower portion of the flue and connecting it with the smoke-box.

The " Black Hawk " rested on four wheels, the driving wheels about four and a half feet diameter, being in front of the fire-box. The guide wheels were about three feet diameter. Inside cylinders were used, and these required a double crank axle, and the latter, forged solid, could not easily be had. Col. Long overcame this difficulty by making his driving axle in three pieces, with two bearings on each, and with separate cranks keyed on to the ends of each portion of the axle, with shackle or crank pins arranged after the manner of the modern side-wheel steamer shafts.

Flanged tires of wrought iron could not then be had easily, and this was overcome in the "Black Hawk," by making the tread for the wheels of two narrow bands, shrunk side by side on the wooden rim, with a flat ring, forming the flange, bolted on the side of the wheel. Springs were only admissable over the front axle, and to save shocks in the rear, the after or fire-box portion of the boiler was suspended upon springs. The camb cut-off, then much in vogue on the engines of the Mississippi steamers, was used in the "Black Hawk." Other locomotives, mainly after the design of the "Black Hawk," were built by Long & Norris, and by William Norris & Co., in 1834, but they were not greatly successful.

With the firm of William Norris & Co. Col. Long retired from the manufacture of locomotives in Philadelphia, and his name was not thereafter heard of in connection with its improvement. On the retirement of Col. Long, William Norris, a gentleman then with no acknowledged pretensions as a mechanic or engineer, brought other skill to his assistance, and after several not very successful efforts with engines of a design more like those that had succeeded of other makers, brought out an engine, in 1836, called the "George Washington," the success of which laid the foundation of the large business done for thirty years thereafter at Bush Hill, Philadelphia, by William Norris, and subsequently by his brother Richard Norris.

THE LOCOMOTIVE ENGINE. 37

The "George Washington" was a six-wheel engine with outside cylinders, having one pair of driving wheels, 4 feet in diameter, forward of the fire-box, with vibrating truck, for turning curves, in front. This engine weighed somewhat over fourteen thousand pounds, and a large proportion of the whole weight rested on the single pair of driving wheels.

This locomotive, when put upon the Columbia road (now Pennsylvania Central), did apparently, the impossible feat of running up the old inclined plane at Peter's Island, 2,800 feet long, with a rise of one foot in fourteen, drawing a load of more than nineteen thousand pounds above the weight of the engine, and this, too, at a speed of fifteen miles per hour. This was no doubt impossible, if the simple elements of the calculation are only considered. But there was a point in this experiment, well known to experts at the time, which *did* make it possible, even by calculation; and this point consisted in the amount of extra weight that was thrown upon the drivers by the action of the draft link connecting the tender with the engine,—the result being that about *all* the weight of the locomotive rested upon the drivers, less the weight of the truck frame and wheels in front. This most extraordinary feat, a writer on the subject says, "took the engineering world by storm, and was hardly credited."

The "George Washington," an heir of the earlier efforts of Col. Long, was unquestionably a good and well made engine, and greatly superior to any that had preceded it from the Norris Works. The fame this engine earned, led to large orders in the United States, and several locomotives of like character were ordered for England and for Germany.

Improvements were made from time to time in the Norris locomotives—the establishment fairly holding its own, with its rivals until the Norris Works ceased to exist about 1866 or '67. Mr. William Norris, who in connection with Col. Long, had founded the works at Philadelphia, at one time commenced the building of locomotives at Vienna, Austria, but with no very great success; and after his return ceased his connection with the Norris Works. At the epoch from 1833 to 1837, the Norris and Baldwin engines had each their advantages and defects.

The Norris engine, as it was at the commencement of 1837, may be described as follows: The boiler was of the dome pattern, known in England as Bury's, and used by that maker in 1830; the framing was of wrought iron. The cylinders were placed outside of, and were fastened to the smoke-box as well as to the frame. The engine was supported on one pair of driving wheels, placed forward of the fire-box, and on a swivelling four-wheeled truck placed under the smoke-box. The centre of the truck being so much in advance of the point of bearing of the leading wheels in the English engines of that day, there was considerably greater weight placed upon the driving wheels in proportion to the whole weight, while it was not unusual to adjust the draw bar so as to throw a portion of the weight of the tender upon the hinder end of the engine when drawing its load. These engines used four excentrics with latches. Hand levers were used for putting the valve rods into gear when standing. The valve motion was efficient, as the performances of these engines fully attested.

The "Baldwin" engine of the same period had a similar boiler, and somewhat similar position of, and fastening of the cylinders. The driving wheels were placed behind the fire-box, the usual truck being placed under the smoke-box. These engines ran steadily, owing to their extended wheel base, although they did not have the weight on the drivers, and the consequent adhesive power of the Norris engine. The framing was of wood covered with iron plates, and was placed outside the wheels.

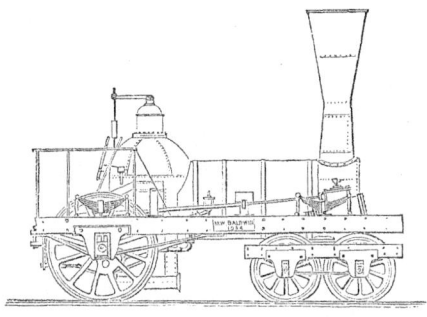

M. W. BALDWIN, 1837.

The driving wheels had two outside bearings. The cylinders, although outside of the smoke-box, were placed so as to give a connection to the crank inside of the driving wheels. The crank was formed in the driving axle, but instead of being made as a complete double or full crank, the neck, to which the connecting rod was attached, was extended through and fastened into a hole in the driving wheel, the

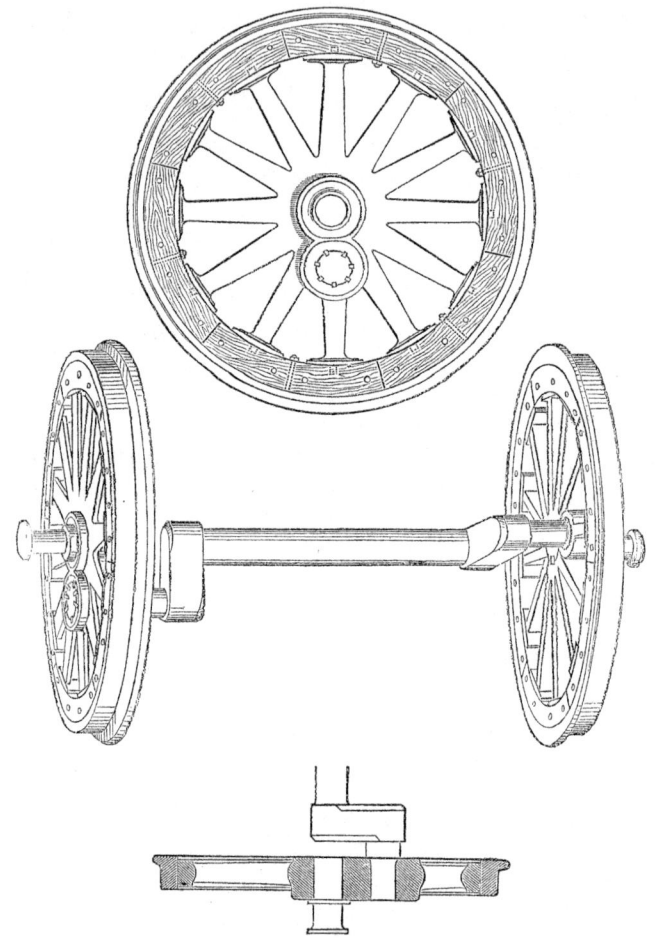

M. W. BALDWIN'S IMPROVED CRANK AXLE, 1834-37.

distance from the centre being equal to the throw of the crank. A simple straight pin, fitted to the centre of the wheel, and extending outwards, formed an outside bearing for the axles. This device of Mr. Baldwin's was most ingenious and efficient. It simplified by more than one-half the making of a crank shaft, and increased its strength, and at the same time caused the thrust of the cylinder to act close to the driving wheel inside, in the same manner as the outside crank pin.

With the introduction of the outside cylinder, this mode of making a crank axle has gone into disuse The guide bar for the cross-head, which had a double V top and bottom, was clasped by the cross-head, and being hollow and with valve-chamber attached, was made to serve the purpose of a force pump. The valve-gear, already described, was placed under the foot-board, and although efficient, was cramped for room, the excentric rods consequently being rather too short.

In workmanship and proportion of parts, the Baldwin engine was the superior of the two class of locomotives that had then become in their manufacture, an important feature in the trade of Philadelphia.

M. W. Baldwin, in 1834 and 1837, had greatly the advantage of the Norris establishment, as he had had from the first, in being a good practical machinist himself, and in having had some experience in steam engine building previous to the making of the "Ironsides," in 1832; whereas, William Norris, after Col. Long retired, in 1833–34, having personally little engineering knowledge and no practical skill in engine building, was left entirely dependent upon hired assistance, which at that time, in the construction of the locomotive, was most difficult if not almost impossible to obtain.

Mr. Baldwin had also the great advantage of better workshops and better tools than his early competitor at the commencement of this new business; hence his success was at once more decided, and the improvements in his locomotives, both in design and in workmanship, were more important from the beginning. It is needless to speak of the "Baldwin Locomotive Works" of to-day.

With a record of forty years, during the early period of which it passed successfully through many vicissitudes, it maintains its well-earned character of the first locomotive manufactory both in quantity and quality, in this country; and it is doubtful whether it is not now the equal to, if not the superior, in these particulars, of any establishment doing similar work in the world.

The Baldwin engine of 1837, with its driving axle behind the fire-box, was steady at high speeds, but with insufficient adhesion to the rails.

The Norris engine, of the same date, having a great proportion of the weight overhanging the driving axle, and having adhesion equal to its cylinder power, was unsteady on the rails. Improvement rested between the two systems of Baldwin and of Norris.

In the spring of 1835, the firm of Garrett & Eastwick, then making steam engines and light machinery in Philadelphia, desiring to engage in this new business, obtained an order for building a locomotive engine for the Beaver Meadow Railroad. This firm, having no practical knowledge of locomotive engine building, had called to their assistance as foreman, Mr. Joseph Harrison, Jr., a young man of twenty-five, with ten years experience in the workshop, and a good practical workman, who had been employed for nearly two years as a journeyman in the Norris works, and who when there had been schooled amidst the indifferent successes or real failures of Long & Norris, and Wm. Norris & Co. The first locomotive designed under the above auspices was called, when finished, the Samuel D. Ingham, after the President of the road. It had outside cylinder connections, then not much in vogue,— running gear after the Baldwin type, with one pair of driving wheels behind the fire box, and with four wheel truck in front. It had the dome or "Bury" boiler.

This engine had some points about it which differed from any locomotive that had preceded it. Its most distinguishing feature was an ingenious and entirely original mode of reversement, invented and patented by Mr. Andrew M. Eastwick, the junior member of the firm. It is scarcely possible to give a correct idea of this device without a model or drawings, but its principle consisted in the introduction of a movable block or slide, called a reversing valve, between the usual slide valve and the opening through the cylinder face. This reversing valve had an opening through it vertically for the exhaust, and two sets of steam openings, corresponding, when placed opposite thereto, to the openings on the cylinder face. One set, called direct openings, passed directly through the valve, and when fixed for going forward, made the usual channels to the cylinder. The second set of openings through the reversing valve, called indirect openings, coming into play when the engine moved backwards, passed from the upper surface of this valve but half way through it, and thence were diverted laterally to the side of the valve, and thence along the side and again laterally, came out of the under side where the reversing valve rested against the valve face of the cylinder, directly opposite a second indirect opening on the upper surface of this valve.

When the reversing valves were fixed for going forward, the direct openings were then exactly over the steam openings on the cylinder, whilst the indirect openings came over the solid surface of the cylinder face, and were entirely out of use. The exhaust opening through the reversing valve in this case, came directly opposite the exhaust opening on the cylinder. The slide valve, never detached from the excentric, moved always over both sets of openings in the usual way. Moving the reversing valve to the opposite end of the steam chest from where it had been placed in going forward, and the case was different, Then, steam, entering the reversing valve at the upper side, instead of going directly into the cylinder as before, was diverted in the manner just described, and came out at the cylinder face at the opposite end from which it had entered on the slide valve face on the upper side of the reversing valve, and thus the direction of the engine was changed from forwards to backwards, or *vice versa*, without detaching or re-attaching any of the moving parts of the valve gear.

The principle and action of Mr. Eastwick's invention may be guessed at from what has been described, although its detail may not be so easily made out.

This new arrangement, neat and efficient as it was, had its defects, which no doubt interfered with its general use. It increased by the thickness of the reversing block, the length of the steam openings, in going forward, and further increased their length in going backwards. It also prevented the use of a long lap on the slide valve, for, any lead of the excentric in going forward, causing a corresponding delay in receiving steam in moving backward. In reviewing these defects, the beauty and originality of Mr. Eastwick's device must not be overlooked.

Nothing for the same purpose, so novel in its mode of action had preceded, or has succeeded this invention of a Philadelphia mechanic, and it is doubtful whether any locomotive has since been made with so few moving parts as this first engine of Garrett & Eastwick. This engine had for the first time, the rear platform covered with a roof to protect the engineman and fireman from the weather.

The success of the "Samuel D. Ingham" was quite equal to any locomotive of its class that had been built up to that period in Philadelphia, and orders came to the makers from several sources for others of the same kind.

In 1836, Henry R. Campbell, of Philadelphia, " in order to distribute the weight of the engine upon the rails more completely," patented the duplication of the driving wheels, placing one pair behind and one pair in front of the fire-box, using the swivelling truck in front, of Baldwin's and others.

Mr. Campbell subsequently made an engine after his patent, which was tried on the Philadelphia and Germantown Railroad, and although not a decided success, it was a great step in the direction in which improvement was most needed. Its principal defect consisted in its having no good means of equalizing the weight on the driving wheels, so as to meet the various undulations in the track.

To remedy the defects in the Baldwin, Campbell and Norris engines, Garrett & Eastwick, (soon thereafter changing their firm to Garrett, Eastwick & Co., Joseph Harrison, Jr., becoming the junior partner), commenced in the winter of 1836-7, a new style of locomotive, for the Beaver Meadow Railroad Company.

Adopting the Campbell plan of running gear, they aimed at making a much heavier engine, for freight purposes, than had yet been used. This could be only rendered possible on the slight roads of the country at that time, by a better distribution of the weight upon the rails.

In the first of the improved engines made by Garrett & Eastwick for the Beaver Meadow Rail-

HENRY R. CAMPBELL'S FIRST DESIGN FOR AN EIGHT-WHEELED LOCOMOTIVE.—1836.

road, Mr. Andrew M. Eastwick introduced an important improvement in the Campbell eight wheel engine, for which he obtained a patent in 1836. This improvement consisted in the introduction under the rear end of the main frame, of a separate frame in which the two axles were placed, one pair before and one pair behind the fire box. This separate frame was made rigid in the " Hercules," the first engine in which it was used, and vibrated upon its centre vertically, and being held together firmly at the ends, both sides at all times moved in the same plane, thus only accommodating the undulations in the track in a perfect manner, when the irregularities were on both rails alike. The weight of the engine rested upon the centre of the sides of this separate frame through the intervention of a strong spring above the main frame, the separate frame being held in place by a pedestal bolted to the main frame, the centres of the separate frame vibrating upon a journal sliding vertically in this pedestal.

Mr. Eastwick's design was, however, somewhat imperfect, in not accommodating the weight of the four driving-wheels to the irregular undulations on both tracks. There were other minor improvements in the " Hercules," one of which was the introduction, for the first time into steam machinery, of the bolted stub-end instead of the old fashioned and unsafe mode of gib and key for holding the strap on the connecting rods. This device, an idea of Mr. Harrison's, is now universally used in the connecting rods of the locomotive engine.

48   THE LOCOMOTIVE ENGINE.

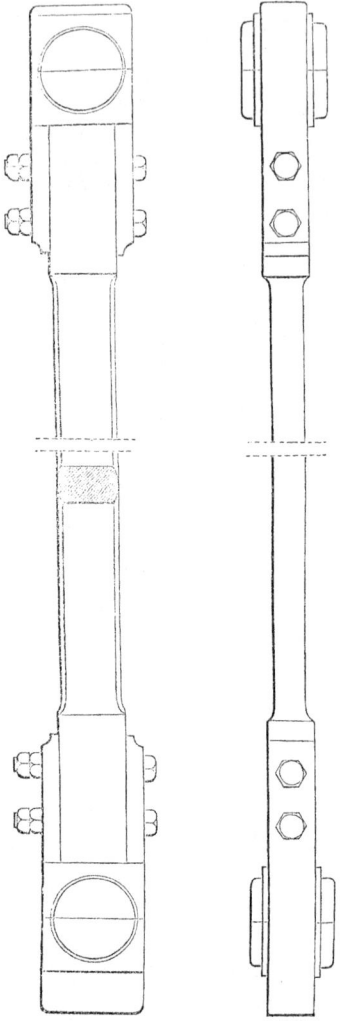

HARRISON'S STUB-END, 1837,
MADE WITHOUT KEYS.

Doubts were expressed by some, and amongst them not a few engine builders, that the "Hercules," weighing about *fifteen tons*, would prove too heavy,—that this engine would not turn curves or go into switches without trouble &c., &c.,—but Eastwick & Harrison had good friends in Captain Mathew C. Jenkins, a director, and Mr. A. Pardee, the chief-engineer of the Beaver Meadow Railroad. They had committed themselves to this new style of locomotive and were not disposed to see it fail for lack of a fair trial. They had no cause to regret their confidence in after years. At the time the "Hercules" was placed upon the Beaver Meadow Railroad, this road had a flat rail, but five-eighths of an inch thick and two and a half inches wide, laid upon continuous string-pieces of wood, with mud-sills underneath.

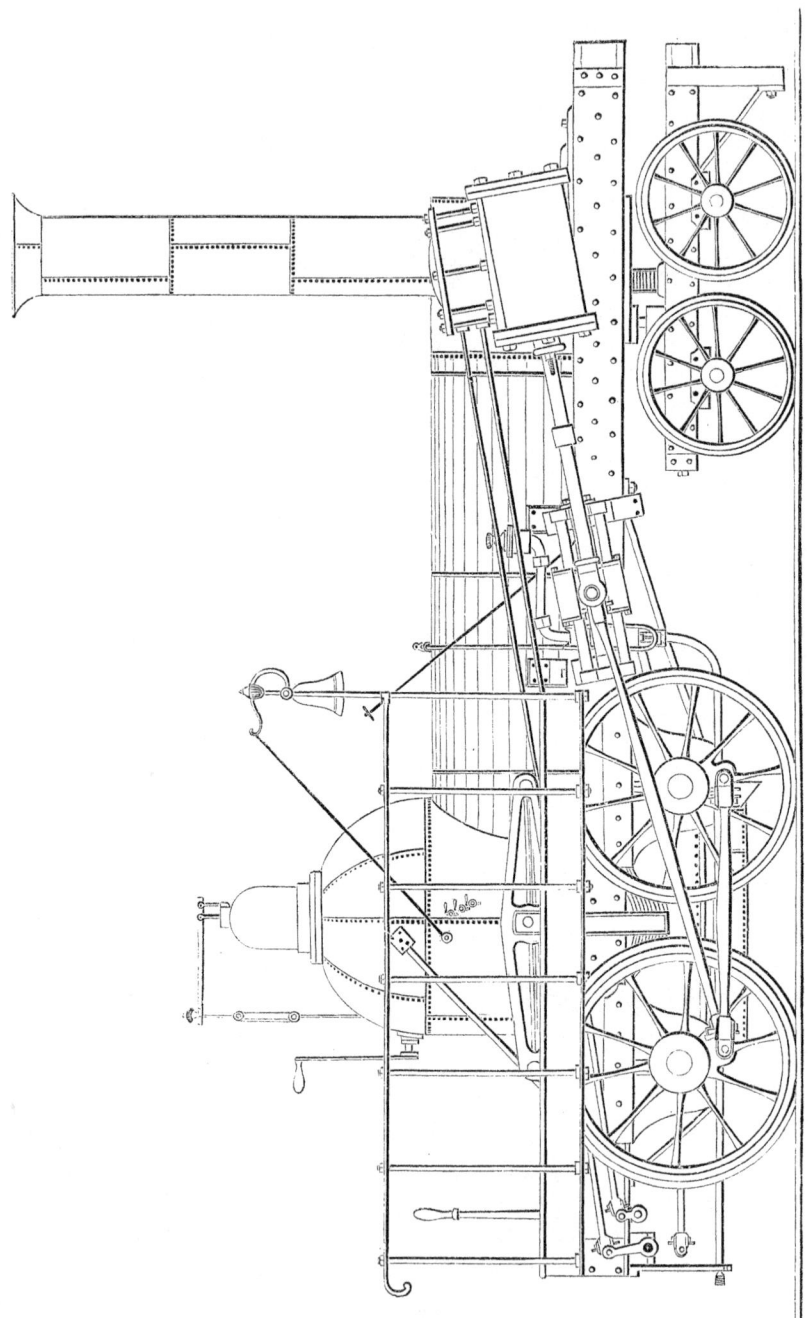

"HERCULES."

Garrett & Eastwick's first eight-wheeled Locomotive.—1837. As arranged with "Harrison" equalizing levers.

The "Hercules," when put in operation on the Beaver Meadow Railroad, proved a great success, and led to other orders for the same class of engine. This division of the weight on more points of the road, and its more perfect equalization thereon, seemed at the time, as it has proved since, to have been the commencement of a new era in the history of the locomotive. To remedy the defect, incident to Mr. Eastwick's plan, as before mentioned, in these early eight wheel engines, an improvement was patented, in 1838, by Joseph Harrison, Jr., the junior partner of the firm of Eastwick & Harrison.

Mr. Harrison's patent showed many ways of carrying out the principle of his improvement, but the one preferred consisted in placing the driving axle bearings in pedestals, in the usual manner, bolted to the main frame, and by the use of a compensating lever above the main frame, vibrating on its centre, at the point of attachment to the main frame, the ends of this lever resting on the axle-boxes by means of pins passing through the frame. These levers vibrated on each side of the engine separately, and thus met all the unevenness in both rails within a certain prescribed limit, which was governed by the play of the axle-boxes in the pedestals.

This arrangement of Mr. Harrison's was simpler, lighter and cheaper than the one that had preceded it, and was used in all the eight wheel engines built by Eastwick & Harrison after the second one.

In all engines now built in this country or in Europe, with more than six wheels, this device of Mr.

Harrison is used in one or other of the different ways indicated in his patent. Mr. Harrison's patent included an improvement in the forward truck, making it flexible so that it would accommodate itself to irregular undulations on both rails.

The engineers and manufacturers of this period, did not at once fully understand the significance of the innovation so successfully carried out by Eastwick & Harrison. They clung to the older idea that one pair of driving wheels was quite sufficient whether placed before the fire-box or behind, nor did they fairly adopt the new system until after its value had been fully demonstrated by several years of trial.

In the summer of 1839, Eastwick & Harrison received an order from the Philadelphia and Reading Railroad Co., through the chief-engineer, Mr. Moncure Robinson, for a freight engine that had peculiar points. This engine was designed generally upon the "Hercules" plan, but it was stipulated in the contract that the whole weight should be *eleven tons* gross, with *nine tons* on the four driving wheels. It was also stipulated that it should burn anthracite coal in a horizontal tubular boiler.

To distribute the nine tons on the driving wheels, the rear axle was placed *under* the fire-box, and somewhat in advance of its central line, instead of being behind the fire-box, as in the "Hercules." This arrangement of the rear axle permitted nine tons of the whole weight of the engine to rest on the four driving wheels. The boiler was of the Bury type, and the fire-box had the then unprecedented length, outside,

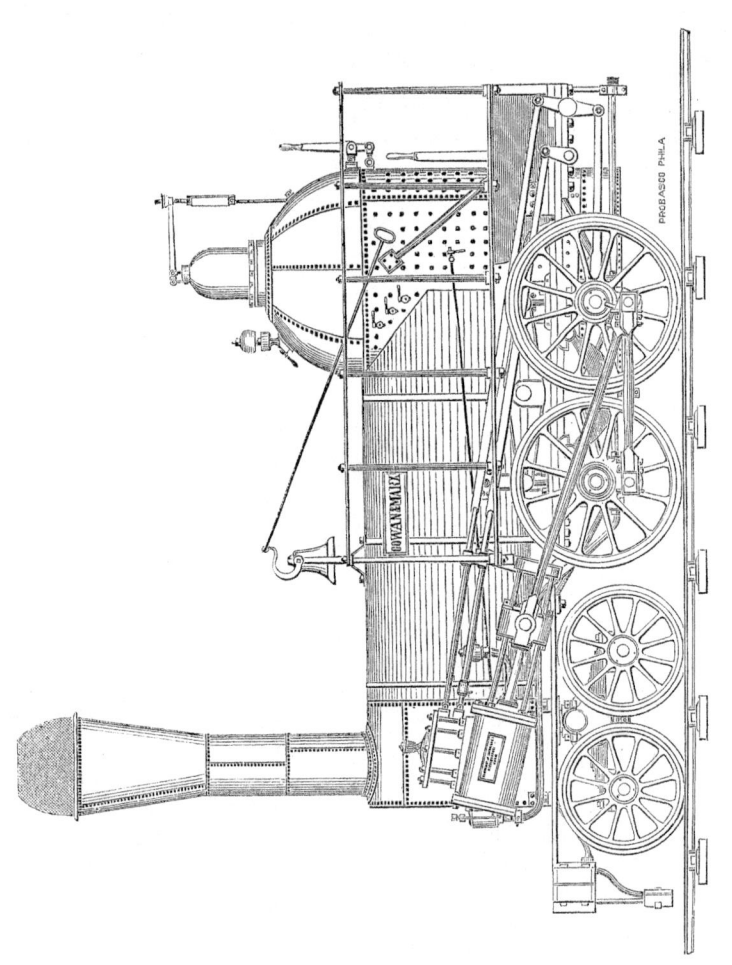

FREIGHT ENGINE "GOWAN & MARX."

Designed and built by Eastwick & Harrison, Philadelphia, for the Philadelphia and Reading Railroad.—1839.
Slightly varied from the original.

of five feet. The tubes, two inches in diameter, and only five feet long, were more numerous than usual, and filled the cylinder part of the boiler almost to the top. Cylinders, $12\frac{1}{2}$ inches in diameter, 18-inch stroke, using no cut-off; driving wheels 42 inches. The Gurney draft-box was used with many exhaust jets, instead of one or two large ones.

It is believed, that in this engine was used for the first time, the steam jet for exciting the fire when standing. The engine here described, called, when finished, the Gowan & Marx, after a London banking firm, excited much attention in the railroad world by its great tractive power, compared with its whole weight.

On one of its trips (February 20th, 1840,) it drew a train of *one hundred and one* four-wheel loaded cars from Reading to Philadelphia, at an average speed of 9.82+ miles per hour, nine miles of the road being a continuous level. The gross load on this occasion was 423 tons, not including the engine and tender, which, if the weight of the tender is counted, equalled *forty times* the weight of the engine.

See "Journal of Franklin Institute," 1840, vol. 25, page 99, Report of G. N. Nicols, Supt. Philadelphia and Reading Railroad, which closes as follows: "The above performance of an eleven ton engine is believed to excel any on record in this or any other country." It may be doubted whether it has been excelled since.

How strangely this feat of the Gowan and Marx compares with the trials on the Liverpool and Manchester Railroad in October, 1829, but ten years before, when all that was required of the competing locomotives was, that they should draw about *three times* their own weight, tender included, on a level track, five miles long, especially prepared for the trial. The great success of the Gowan and Marx, induced the Philadelphia and Reading Railroad Company to duplicate the plan of this engine in ten engines subsequently built at Lowell, Mass.

In 1840, the Gowan and Marx attracted the particular attention of the Russian engineers, Colonels Melnikoff and Krafft, who had been commissioned by the Emperor Nicholas to examine into and report upon the various systems of railroads and railroad machinery, then in operation in this country and in Europe.

The result of their examination was favorable to the American system, and when the engineers above named, made their report on the construction of a railroad from St. Petersburg to Moscow, an engine upon the plan of the Gowan and Marx, was recommended as best adapted to the purposes of this first great line of railroad in the Empire of Russia, and Eastwick and Harrison were requested to visit St. Petersburg with the view of making a contract for building the locomotives and other machinery for the road.

Mr. Harrison went to St. Petersburg in the spring of 1843, and in connection with Mr. Thomas Winans, of Baltimore, a contract was concluded with the government of Russia, at the close of the same year,

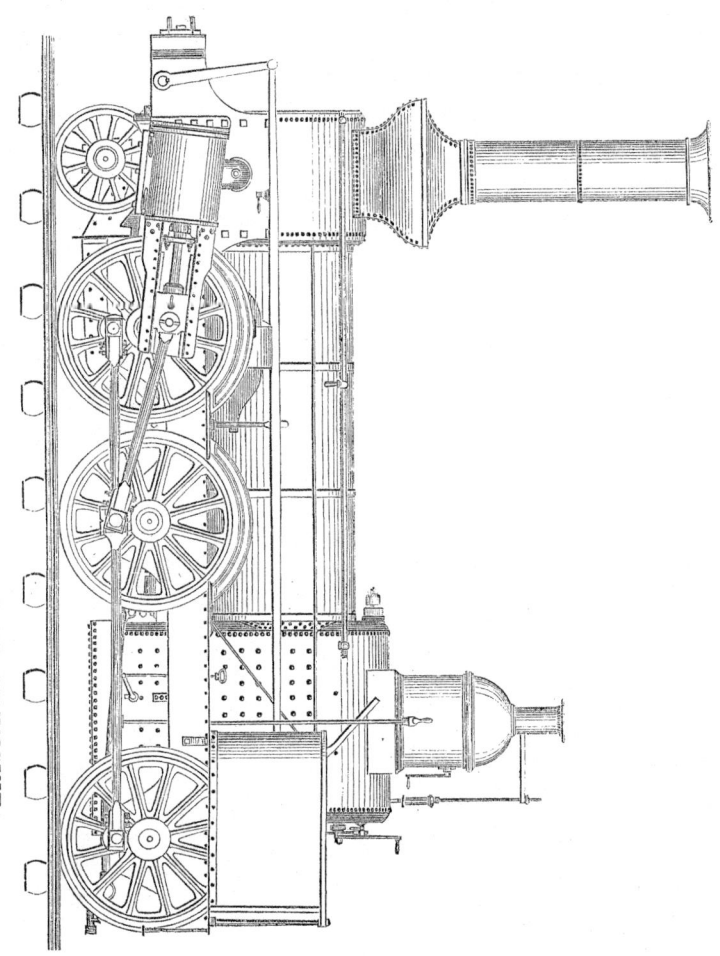

HARRISON, WINANS & EASTWICK'S FREIGHT ENGINE.
Built at St. Petersburgh, Russia, for the St. Petersburgh and Moscow Railroad.—1844.

Freight Engine, Matthew Baird & Co., Baldwin Locomotive Works, 1872.

for building 162 locomotives, and iron trucks for 2,500 freight cars. Mr. Eastwick joined Mr. Harrison and Mr. Winans at St. Petersburg in 1844.

Eastwick & Harrison closed their establishment in Philadelphia in 1844, removing a portion of their tools and instruments to St. Petersburg, and there, under the firm of Harrison, Winans & Eastwick, completed, at the Alexandroffsky Head Mechanical Works, the work for which they had contracted. When the work was commenced under the contract of Harrison, Winans & Eastwick with the Russian government, Joseph Harrison, Jr., designed and had built under his own supervision, at St. Petersburgh, the first machine, it is believed, that was ever made for boring out the holes for right-angled crank pins in the driving wheels of locomotive engines. This right-angled boring machine, on precisely the same principle as devised by Mr. Harrison, has since become indispensable in every locomotive establishment. The same idea was partially put in use as early as 1838, when the second eight-wheel engine "Beaver" was built by Garrett & Eastwick for the Beaver Meadow Railroad.

The first contract with the Russian government was closed in 1851, at which time a second contract was entered into, by two members of the firm, for the repairs to the rolling stock of the St. Petersburg and Moscow Railroad, which continued until 1862.

The eight-wheel locomotive of Eastwick & Harrison, made its first reputation as a freight engine. In 1842, two were built by this firm for the Baltimore and Ohio Railroad, which were specially designed for running passenger trains at extra fast speed.

One of these engines, the "Mercury," during the year 1844, ran the large aggregate of 37,000 miles, which, by the annual report of the Baltimore and Ohio road for that year, is assumed to be the largest result on record up to that time.

From what has been here stated, it will be seen that the new system of engine had won fame in both freight and passenger service, but even as late as 1844, it had not established itself in the estimation of some of the best locomotive engine builders in the country. In November, 1838, M. W. Baldwin wrote to a correspondent " that he did not think there was any advantage in the eight-wheeled engine. There being three points in contact, it could not turn a curve, he argued, without slipping one or the other pair of wheels sideways. Another objection was in the multiplicity of machinery and the difficulty in maintaining four driving wheels all of exactly the same size." He however, in 1845, bought the patent-right for this plan of engine of Mr. H. R. Campbell, and the patent for the equalizing beam between the drivers, of Messrs. Eastwick & Harrison, and delivered to the South Carolina Railroad Company, in December, 1845, his first eight-wheeled engine with four drivers and a four-wheeled truck. " With the completion of the first eight-wheeled " C " engine, Mr. Baldwin's feelings underwent a revulsion in favor of this plan, and his

IMPROVEMENTS OF M. W. BALDWIN.

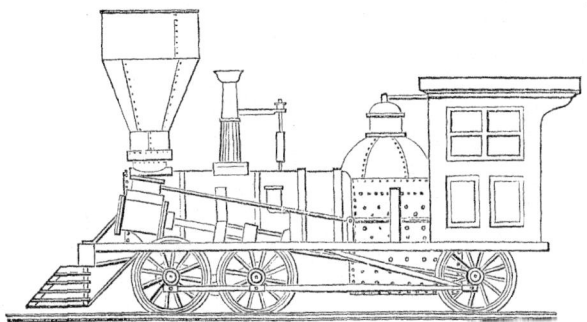

BALDWIN'S SIX-WHEEL CONNECTED ENGINE.—1842.

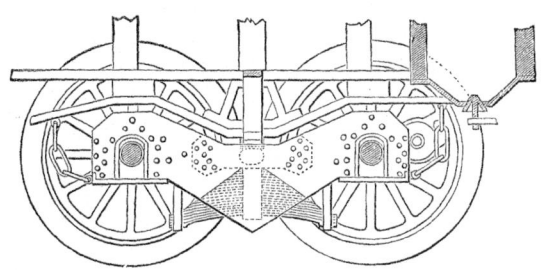

FLEXIBLE BEAM TRUCK.—1842.

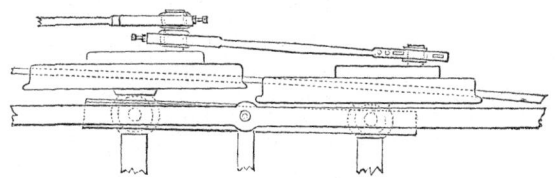

HALF-PLAN OF FLEXIBLE BEAM TRUCK.

Standard Passenger Engine, made by M. Baird & Co.   BALDWIN LOCOMOTIVE WORKS.   Philadelphia: 1872.

partiality for it became as great as had been his antipathy before. Commenting on the machine, he recorded himself as more pleased with its appearance and action than any engine he had turned out."

In the "Mercury" was introduced for the first time, the single long spring, forming the side pieces of the forward truck frame, with journal boxes for the axles at the ends, and journal bearings in the middle of the springs, fitted to, and vibrating on the ends of a wrought iron bolster, with the whole weight of the forward part of the engine resting on the centre of the bolster.

The locomotive of the " Hercules " type, and those that immediately followed it from the same makers, is the standard passenger engine in this country, no other being now used, and it has been introduced in Europe for the same purpose. It is no longer generally used as a freight engine. In the years immediately succeeding the making of the Gowan and Marx, it was found that much more than nine tons distributed on four driving wheels was needed for adequate adhesion to the rails, and hence the introduction of six, and even eight connected driving wheels sometimes used with the addition of the forward truck.

Following the early efforts of Baldwin, Norris, Campbell and Eastwick and Harrison, other Philadelphia engineers and machinists entered the field in the manufacture and improvement of the locomotive. Mr. Henry R. Campbell built several very creditable six-wheel engines. James Brooks & Co., aided by Mr. Samuel Wright, a fellow apprentice of Joseph Harrison, Jr., in the workshop of Hyde & Flint, Kensington, a young man of good practical skill, constructed a locomotive which had several new points worthy of notice. Its running gear was after the type of the six-wheel engine of Baldwin, with one pair of driving wheels behind the fire-box, and with outside cylinder connections. The cross-head slides were made in the form of a cylinder, bored out and arranged to serve the purpose of feed-pumps, the cross-head forming the piston of the pump. The connecting-rod entered the lower or open end of the slide, which was large enough to allow clearance at the angles of the rod. The usual valve chamber was placed at the upper end of the slide and thence a pipe led to the boiler. This mode of arranging a feed-pump was more ingenious in design than useful in practice, and was not repeated in a second engine built by the same makers.

Another new point in the Wright engine was the mode of reversement, which was the same in principle as the Costell plan. The slide valve was open through the top, from the exhaust cavity underneath, and terminated in a cylindric form in which was fitted a metallic spring-piston closing up the opening through the valve. When the engine was going forward, steam from the boiler entered the steam chest, and the slide valve acted in the usual manner.

When going backward, by the peculiar arrangement of a slide valve which acted also as a steam or

LOCOMOTIVE "MERCURY," BUILT BY EASTWICK & HARRISON, FOR THE BALTIMORE & OHIO RAILROAD, 1842.

throttle valve, the steam from the boiler, by a process similar to a two-way cock, was turned under the cylinder slide valve and into the cavity of the exhaust, forcing the piston in the top of the valve, upward and against the evenly planed under surface of the steam chest lid, the exhaust pipe becoming the steam chest, and the steam chest the exhaust pipe, and *vice versa*, when the movement of the engine had to be changed.

This mode of the throttle valve and reversement valve in one, combined with the piston slide valve, was a most simple and certain arrangement. It had, with Costell's, the same defect in the matter of the lead of the slide valve as the "Eastwick" mode of reversement.

Eastwick & Harrison made two locomotives in 1838, with vibrating valves moving on faces on the side of fixed cylinders, reversing Costell's plan. In these two engines the throttle valve and reverse were combined in the same manner as in the Wright and in the Costell engine, by the movement of a slide valve moving over three openings.

With the second engine of James Brooks & Co., also designed by Samuel Wright, an attempt was made to secure the adhesion of the forward swivelling truck wheels in combination with one pair of driving wheels behind the fire-box, which worked with fair practical success. This same idea was carried out by Mr. Baldwin at, or near this period.

James Brooks & Co. did not continue the building of locomotives after this second trial.

About this time, Messrs. Charles and Escoll Sellers, of the firm of Coleman Sellers & Sons, of Philadelphia, built a locomotive somewhat after the plan of the Baldwin engine. It is not remembered that this engine had any specially original points except in the arrangement of the draw-link between the engine and tender, whereby the point of attachment to the engine could be raised or lowered, so as to bring more or less of the weight of the tender for increasing the adhesion of the driving wheels.

Mr. Escoll Sellers, some years later than this, invented and patented the plan of central rail, with vertical friction rollers, the same as has been used up to a recent period on the "Fell" railroad crossing, Mont Cenis, before the completion of the tunnel.

Edward Young at Newcastle, Delaware, and Leonard Phleger, Philadelphians, also made improvements in the locomotive.

In 1846, Septimus Norris, a brother of Wm. Norris, patented a ten wheel locomotive with six driving wheels, combined with swivelling truck forward. Several of these engines were built for the Philadelphia and Reading Railroad.

It is true that from amongst all these pioneers in the manufacture and improvement of the locomotive engine, the Baldwin Locomotive Works only remains in Philadelphia at this time.

But the fact, that the smaller establishments exist no longer, should not cause the workers in the early day to be forgotten. They helped to attract the attention of the railway world towards Philadelphia as the

HARRISON, WINANS & EASTWICK'S PASSENGER ENGINE.

Built at St. Petersburgh, Russia, for the St. Petersburgh and Moscow Railroad.—1844.

IMPROVEMENTS OF M. W. BALDWIN.

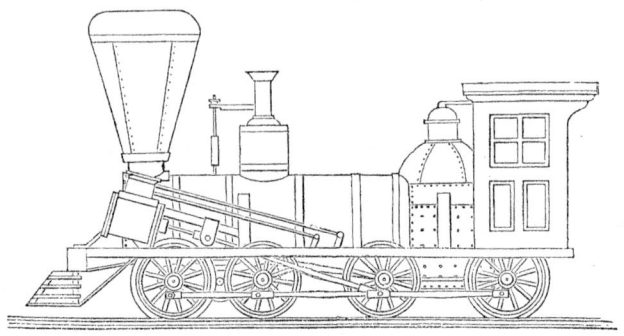

BALDWIN'S EIGHT-WHEEL CONNECTED ENGINE.—1846.

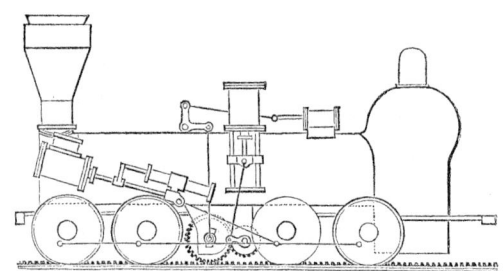

BALDWIN'S ENGINE FOR RACK RAIL.—1847.

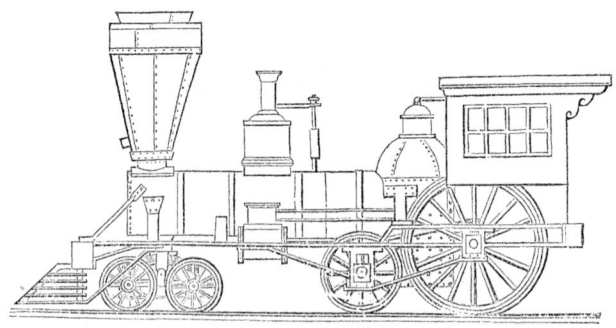

BALDWIN'S FAST MESSENGER ENGINE. 1848.

great source of supply for railroad machinery, and in this they helped also to make it possible for us to have to-day, the great locomotive establishment, which is now the pride and boast of Philadelphia.

The eight-wheel engine of Campbell,—first built by him in 1836, and with the added improvements of Eastwick and Harrison in 1836 and 1837, subsequently copied by Baldwin, Norris and all other makers, is to-day, after more than thirty years of trial, with but little change except in minor detail, and in its greatly increased weight,—the passenger locomotive of this country.

Baldwin, Norris and others, did much toward the improvement of the freight engine, and have earned a well-merited reputation in its construction. These improvements in the freight and passenger engine culminated, in a great degree, about 1843, and little has since been done, tending towards important changes in the present system. It is however fairly possible, notwithstanding the improvements that have been made in the freight engine since 1843, in the increase of its number of driving wheels and its greater weight, that the locomotive engine that is to do the heavy transport of the world, has not yet been made. It would seem that but little improvement can be looked for in the present system. If improvements of any great importance are to be made in this class of locomotive in the future, they must be looked for in a "new departure" which may in no small degree ignore nearly all that has been done heretofore.

In tracing this history from the date of Colonel

Long's first effort to the period at which the locomotive has reached its present perfection, it cannot but be noted how persistently and tenaciously Philadelphia mechanics and engineers clung to the early idea of making an engine that should have important original traits, and it is further remarkable that in no single instance has there been even a desire to merely repeat what had been done elsewhere.

Take the best locomotives now made in the United States, and it will be difficult to find one that has not upon it some distinct impress of a Philadelphia mechanic, and it may be fairly claimed that they have made a mark upon this most important and useful machine that is eminently Philadelphian.

In the long future when the story of the locomotive is inquired into and rehearsed by the curious, as it will be, Philadelphia's honor, fairly earned, will not be overlooked, nor should the names of those who have aided in earning this honor be forgotten.

The story has now been told of what Philadelphia engineers and mechanics have done at home, in the early and later day, in the development and improvement of the locomotive engine. This record would not be complete without some reference is made to that which they have done outside of Philadelphia.

These workers can be found everywhere, and for nearly forty years Philadelphia skill has been sought for to fill responsible places in all parts of the United States, in the West Indies, in South America and in Europe, and even in British India.

THE LOCOMOTIVE ENGINE. 61

It is not only in the improvement of the locomotive that Philadelphia engineers and mechanics excel, but they are widely known and appreciated as the designers and manufacturers of all other kinds of railroad machinery. They are particularly noted for perfection in machines and instruments used in building the locomotive engine.

The ordinary observer, in looking at the perfect locomotive of the present day, and the perfect means in material and in instruments, which render it now so easy to make it what it is, bestows little thought upon the amount of labor, both of brain and body, that has been expended in bringing it to this perfection. It is plain from the record, that there was no Royal road to the end attained.

The story of the railroad, has been told in part in this history, and it is shown in how little estimation it was held up to near the close of the decade ending with 1830. Its present value is patent to every one, and it looms up as something so vast as almost to disarm discussion. But this value remained almost entirely latent from the time the first iron rail was laid down in Great Britain until the " Rocket " fired this dormant spark in 1829. From that time the railroad took the place it fills to-day, a result only made possible by the little machine that we now see glinting in the sunlight as it crosses field and meadow with its lengthened train,—that we hear in the darkness of midnight, and that even now is threading its way through the dark recesses of the Alpine tunnel, with a mile of rock above its head, making it possible to change the dreary cold of winter to the summer glow of an Italian sky, in less than one short hour. It is this little machine which never tires in its work, and which we never tire in the looking at; towards which the student turns from his books, the ploughman stays his team,—and the mechanic,—the mother and the playful child, stop in their pursuits, to gaze and wonder as it passes by,—not once or twice,—but ever, as it speeds along, they stop and wonder as at something new and strange, and never seen before,—it is this wondrous steed,

> "With iron nerves, and lungs of fire,"

that has made the railroad what it is, that has won this triumph over Time and Space.

Philadelphia, Dec., 1871.

APPENDIX.

Lines to a Locomotive.

WRITTEN ABOUT 1840.

By Hon. Wm. D. Lewis, of Philadelphia, and first published in the first number of the Philadelphia Evening Bulletin.

Sublimest courser of the plain,
  Whom toil can neither daunt, nor tire,
Onward thou bear'st thy lengthened train,
  With Iron nerves and lungs of Fire.

Boldest exploit of daring man,
  Whose restless and impatient mind,
Infringes Nature's general plan.
  And leaves with thee the Winds behind.

No match for thee in airy race,
  The Eagle, borne on sounding wings,
Envying he views thy Lightning pace,
  Most wondrous of Earth's wondrous things.

As some bright Meteor of the sky,
  Or some unsphered and shooting star,
Thou, Locomotive, seems to fly,
  Beheld by dazzled eyes afar.

Science and skill their aid impart,
  Trained, hills to level, valleys rear,
Thy pathway smoothed by laboring art,
  To urge thee in thy swift career.

On then, Majestic, Mighty Steed,
  Speed thy fast flight from clime to clime.
To thee, the glorious task decreed,
  To cancel Space, to vanquish Time.

OCEAN STEAMSHIPS *versus* SAILING SHIPS.

It seems natural that a comparison should be made between the practical value of the steamship for transport on the ocean, and the Locomotive for transport on land. The value of the latter, nay, its absolute necessity, in the onward march of human progress, needs no argument at this day to render it patent to every civilized mind. Can so much be said of the ocean steamers, now so rapidly taking the place of the sailing ship? Let this question be examined for a moment. The boundless ocean, illimitable in its capacity as a highway between continents and nations, had met all the wants and had done its share of the world's work well, from the earliest dawn of maratime trade, up to the period of the advent of the ocean steamer. Its roadway, always in order, except when disturbed by storms,—the power needed for the movement of fleets which, with scarce a stretch of the imagination, might be in the future almost counted as numberless, was furnished by nature's lavish hand, without cost or stint. Necessity, did not demand a better mode as in the case of transport on land, than had been secured by the modern improvements in the sailing ship, making it almost a perfect thing of its kind. So perfect, that even to-day with the steamship altogether in the ascendant, and the best class of sailing ships gone almost entirely out of use, the sailing ship is still the cheaper mode of ocean transport, when all things are taken into the account. And what is the great result that the ocean steamer has achieved? A reduction of a little more than half the time, with greater certainty of arrival, is all that has really been won over wind and sails. It may be a question whether this greater speed, and this greater certainty of arrival is worth what it costs. The rapid exhaustion, and the rapidly increasing ratio in the exhaustion of the coal fields of the world, may, in the not long future, answer this question in the negative.

J. H. Jr.

Report on Eastwick & Harrison's Eight Wheel Locomotives.

The Committee on Science and the Arts, constituted by the Franklin Institute of the State of Pennsylvania, for the promotion of the Mechanic Arts, to whom was referred for examination, Messrs. Eastwick & Harrison's Eight-Wheel Locomotives, Report:—

That these engines possess two peculiarities of an important character, one in the arrangement of the driving wheels, and the other in the mode of maintaining the fire draught.

It is well known to engineers, that the efficiency of the locomotive engine depends, first, upon the quantity of steam which the boiler may be capable of generating in a given time, and secondly, on the amount of friction, or, as it is technically termed, adhesion, between the driving wheels and the road. As the adhesion increases with the weight, it is evident that the engine becomes more effective by increasing its weight, and by throwing a greater proportion of this weight on the drivers.

But a limit to this increase of weight arises from the incapacity of the road to sustain the great pressure thus thrown on a small bearing surface.

To obviate this difficulty, engines have been made with all the wheels coupled so as to constitute them all drivers, and thus distribute the *adhesive* pressure over a greater extent of the road.

Engines of this description are used for heavy and slow draught, but are considered unsafe, from their liability to be thrown off the track at curves.

Another plan, patented a few years back by an engineer of this city, Mr. Henry R. Campbell, was to use four drivers, and at the same time to carry the front end of the engine on a guide truck, as in the six-wheeled engine. But here a new difficulty arose in consequence of the engine having three points of bearing in the line of the rails, on which its weight could not be properly distributed, unless the road was entirely free from irregularities of surface; a condition not to be found on any of the roads which have come under the notice of the Committee.

The improvement invented by Messrs. Eastwick & Harrison is designed to obviate this difficulty, by giving to the eight-wheel engine only two bearing points, one on the guide truck, and the other on a frame supported by the driving wheels. The axles of the drivers are placed one in front, and the other behind the fire-box, and are confined between pedestals of the usual form, fixed to the main frame of the engine, which allow vertical play, but prevent any horizontal motion.

The bearing pins instead of abutting against springs fixed to the frame in the ordinary manner, are jointed to the extremities of horizontal beams of cast iron, one of which is placed on each side of the engine.

To the centre of these beams or levers, are jointed wrought iron rods, which pass down through the engine frame, and carry the springs which support the weight of the engine. The connecting rod of the piston is attached to the hinder

THE LOCOMOTIVE ENGINE. 69

wheel, and this communicates motion to the front driver by a coupling rod attached by a ball and socket joint.

It is evident that this arrangement will allow to each driving wheel, an independent vertical motion, with the advantage that the engine will partake of only one-half the vertical motion of either wheel, in consequence of being suspended at the centre of the horizontal sustaining beam.

The front drivers are without flanches, in order to avoid any difficulty in turning curves.

The peculiarity in the means of maintaining the firedraught, is an apparatus for equalizing the effect of the exhaust steam in the smoke stack, somewhat similar to Gurney's contrivance.

Instead of exhausting directly into the stack, the exhaust steam enters two copper chests, one connected with each cylinder, and escapes from these into the chimney through a number of small tubes.

With the aid of this contrivance, the anthracite fire is kept in a state of intense activity, and generates an abundance of steam, without the annoyance and danger arising from the smoke and sparks of a wood fire.

The heat of the anthracite fire has been found so great as to melt down the grate bars of cast iron which were used in the first experiments with this fuel.

Messrs. E. & H. have since substituted grooved wrought iron bars, which are protected from the action of the fire by a coating of clay placed within the grooves.

A trial of one of these engines on the road between Broad Street and Peter's Island, was witnessed by several members of the Committee on the 25th of April last.

It happened unfortunately, on that occasion, that the business of the road did not furnish so many cars as were desirable for a fair experiment.

The particulars so far as made known to the Committee, were as follows:

Weight of engine, 28,350 lbs. Weight on drivers, 18,059 lbs.
Cylinders, 12 inches diameter. Steam, 90 lbs. to square inch.
Length of stroke, 18 inches. Driving wheels, 44 inches diameter.

The train consisted of 32 loaded cars, estimated at 5 tons each, 2 empty cars weighing 9800 lbs., and tender, 5 tons, making a total of 169 tons. This train was started with great ease on a rising grade and drawn to the foot of the inclined plane, the distance being about 3 miles, with several short curves, and the road in such bad condition as to keep the sustaining beam in continual vibration.

A few days after this experiment, one member of the Committee had an opportunity of witnessing a more decisive trial of the power of the engine.

On the latter occasion, the train consisted of 34 single cars, estimated at five tons each; 4 double cars, 10 tons each; one of Mr. Dougherty's iron boats, 50 tons, and the tender, 5 tons; total, 265 tons.

This train was started without difficulty, on the same rising grade, and drawn over the short curves with apparent ease, with steam blowing off during the whole trip.

This highly interesting experiment was brought to a close somewhat abruptly after proceeding about 2 miles, by the breaking down of one of the cars near the middle of the train.

Although this accident abridged the trial of the power of the engine for draught, it afforded an opportunity of displaying another excellent trait in its performance, this was the facility of reversing* while under way.

As soon as the accident happened, a person stationed on the after part of the train passed a signal to the engineer,

---

*For a report on this mode of reversing, see Journal of Franklin Institute, vol. xviii., p. 179.

THE LOCOMOTIVE ENGINE. 71

the latter immediately reversed the engine and brought the enormous moving mass to a stand, before it had run half its own length. The satisfactory character of the experiments detailed above is sufficient to enable any one who is conversant with transportation on rail roads, to form a correct opinion of the merits of this engine. The impression of those members of the Committee who witnessed the trials, is that it is well adapted for the use of anthracite as fuel, and for very heavy draught; with less tendency to injure the road or to receive injury on a bad road than engines of the usual construction.

By Order of the Committee,

WILLIAM HAMILTON, *Actuary.*

May 9, 1839.

At the request of Messrs. Eastwick & Harrison, the Committee insert the following letter from A. Pardee, Jr., Esq., Engineer of the Beaver Meadow Railroad in reply to their letter requesting information relative to the construction of the road and the performance of their engines upon it. COM. PUB.

Hazleton, Pa., June 8th, 1839.

MESSRS. EASTWICK & HARRISON,

Gentlemen.—I have received yours requesting information as to the construction, &c., of the roads in this region, on which your eight-wheeled locomotives are employed.

The Beaver Meadow Railroad, where one of those engines has been in use two years, has an iron plate rail of $2\frac{1}{4}$ by $\frac{5}{8}$ inches; the wooden rails or string-pieces are oak, a portion 5×7, the remainder 5×8 inches; where the 5×7 rails are used, the cross ties are placed three feet from centre to centre, where the 5×8 they are four feet. The cross ties are laid on plank mud-sills, $2\frac{1}{2}$ inches thick by 10 to 12 inches wide. The shortest curve has a radius of 300 feet; length about 200; but at the foot of the inclined planes, there is a curve around which the engines now daily pass, the radius of which is 250 feet, the length about 300. The heaviest grade is 96 feet per mile, at two points about $\frac{3}{4}$ mile each, there is an average grade of 80 feet per mile, for 5 miles—on the heaviest grade the shortest curve is 550 feet radius, the length about 400 feet. The Hazleton Railroad, on which two of your eight-wheel engines are now in use, has a plate rail $2\frac{1}{4}$ by $\frac{5}{8}$ inches, the string pieces are yellow pine 5×9 inches, the cross ties 4 feet apart, from centre to centre, the mud-sills $2\frac{1}{2}$ by ten to twelve inches. The heaviest grade is 140 feet per mile for $1\frac{1}{2}$ miles; this part of the road was not intended when made, for the use of locomotive power, but it was found in practice that by doubling our trips we could use the engines with more economy than horse power. In regard to the effect on the road, so far as my experience goes, and I have seen the two classes of engines in daily use for more than two years, I would say that the eight-wheel engine was easier on the road than a six-wheel engine of the ordinary construction, with the same weight on the two driving wheels as on each pair of the driving wheels of the eight-wheeled.

There are now in use on the Beaver Meadow and Hazleton Railroads, seven locomotive engines with horizontal tubular boilers, in which anthracite coal is exclusively used as a fuel, after the first fire in the morning, and that we continue to use it when we can have wood for the cost of cutting, is sufficient evidence that we find it to our advantage. We have the Hercules at work and so far, she performs well, running around the curves with great ease.

Respectfully yours,
A. Pardee, Jr.

THE LOCOMOTIVE ENGINE.

Statement of the Performance of the Locomotive Engine, "*Gowan & Marx*," built by Messrs. Eastwick & Harrison, Philadelphia, on the Philadelphia and Reading Railroad, with a train of one hundred and one loaded cars, February 20th, 1840.

Gross weight of train, including cars and freight, but not including engine or tender, 423 tons of 2240 lbs. Net weight of freight, 268½ tons of 2240 lbs. The freight consisted of 2002 barrels of flour, 82 barrels of whiskey, 459 kegs of nails, 19 tons of bar iron, 22 hhds. of meal, 5 hhds. of whiskey, 4 hhds. of oil, and sundry other articles, making a total of 268½ tons.

Distance from Reading to the foot of the Inclined Plane on the Columbia Railroad, 54½ miles. Running time of the engine with train, five hours thirty-three minutes; rate 9.82 miles per hour. Coal consumed, red ash anthracite, from Schuylkill County, 5600 lbs. Water evaporated, 2774 gallons.

GRADES OF ROAD.

The total fall from Reading to the point where the train was stopped near the Columbia Railroad is 214.5 feet, being an average fall of 3.94 feet per mile. There is no ascending grade from Reading to the Columbia Railroad, with the exception of about 2100 feet at its lower termination, graded at 26.4 feet per mile, upon which grade the train was stopped; the other grades vary from 19 to 15 feet per mile; there is only one three miles graded at 18 feet, and one at 19 feet per mile.

The total length of DEAD LEVEL line from Reading to the Columbia Railroad is 27 miles and 4200 feet; of this, the longest level is 9 miles and 500 feet long, between Norristown and the Inclined Plane; the others vary from 1550 feet to 4 miles and 1600 feet in length.

State of the Track.

Owing to the frost coming out of the ground at this season, the track was in worse order than at any other time of the year; this, however, did not materially affect the performance of the engine, as the embankments were all in nearly as good order as at other times, and at comparatively few points in the deep cut was the track sufficiently out of line or level to offer increased resistance to the train.

The superstructure of the road consists of a T rail, 45 lbs. to the yard, laid upon sills 7 feet long and 7 by 8 inches square, 3 feet 1½ inches apart from centre to centre, and laid on broken stone.

State of the Rails.

For the first twenty miles the rails were in very bad order, the morning was cloudy, and the fog of the previous night had left sufficient moisture on the surface of the rails to diminish considerably the adhesion of the engine; for the remainder of the distance the weather was clear and the rails in good order.

Working of the Engine.

On three different occasions the engine started the whole train on a dead level, and when on a dry rail, without the wheels slipping. The steam ranged from 80 lbs. to 130 lbs. per square inch, to which latter pressure the safety-valve was screwed down. The draught of the engine was created by the escape steam passing into, and from a tubed exhaust box, no other draught was used while running. At the water stations, "Reilley's Patent Fan" was used when fresh coal was thrown on the fire, but at no other time. The speed of the train was noted when passing through some curves of 819 feet radius on the 9 mile level, and found to be 9.8

miles per hour; on a straight line, on the same level the engine attained a speed of 10.5 miles per hour. So little was the engine affected by her performance on the 20th, that on the 23d she drew, on her return trip, 88 burden cars, 9 of which were loaded, and a locomotive engine, making a gross weight of 163 tons of 2240 lbs., not including engine or tender, up a grade of 18.4 feet per mile. The train had a strong head wind against it during the whole trip, which, owing to its length, 1206 feet, was sensibly felt at some exposed points of the road, and must have proportionably affected the power of the engine.

WEIGHT AND DIMENSIONS OF THE ENGINE, "GOWAN & MARX."

Weight when empty, 21,640 lbs.; in running order, with fuel and water, 24,660 lbs.; on four driving wheels in running order, or with water, fuel and two men, 18,260 lbs. Cylinders $12\frac{2}{3}$ by 16-inch stroke; 8 wheels, four of which are driving wheels, coupled, 3 feet 4 inches diameter; truck wheels, 2 feet 6 inches diameter. The weight of the burden cars averaged from 1.5 to 1.65 tons of 2240 lbs. each; they were all four-wheeled—wheels 3 feet diameter, and 4 feet 6 inches apart from centre to centre. The above performance of an 11 ton engine, is believed to exceed any on record in this or any other country.

G. N. NICOLLS,
Superintendent Transportation, Phila. & Reading R. R.
Reading, February 24th, 1840.

Letter from Charles Moering, Esq., Engineer to Messrs. Eastwick & Harrison, Locomotive Builders, corner of Twelfth and Willow Streets, Philadelphia.

Gentlemen:—In complying with your request to give you my opinion about your Locomotive Engines, I feel called upon to state the grounds that make this opinion what it is.

I do this in view of the interests of science, not intending to pass a mere encomium upon the productions of your establishment. Every engineer is, no doubt, conversant with the fact, that the power of a locomotive engine not only depends on the harmonious proportions of boiler and cylinders, and on the clever mechanical arrangement to work the pistons and transfer motion to the driving wheels; but every engineer must be also aware of the importance of another fact, viz: the manner in which this power is made available in order to draw a maximum load, at a maximum speed, on a railroad.

In examining this point, we find that a fulcrum is required to enable the steam power to act upon the weight, or the load to be drawn. This fulcrum in the locomotive engine, is evidently the grip of the driving wheels on the rails, meaning the friction between both, or adhesion, as it is technically called.

Let a locomotive engine be ever so powerful, but take away the aforesaid friction, and the wheels will slip, the engine will draw nothing. This adhesion, derived from the pressure of the weight of the engine, must, therefore, bear a certain proportion to the latter. Its maximum will be obtained by throwing the largest, its minimum by placing the smallest amount of the engine's weight on the driving wheels. The minimum, however, has at no time been a desideratum, as the largest amount of adhesion is required for enabling

THE LOCOMOTIVE ENGINE.   77

an engine of a given power to draw a maximum load at a maximum speed.

In the six-wheeled American engine (the true offspring of American mechanical talent, as possesing a fore truck, which affords a most opportune facility for turning curves), there is but one axle to bear the aforesaid proportion of weight; and this axle is the driving axle. On its position, therefore, depended the amount of weight to be made available for producing friction. As it was found impossible as well as improper in practice to place this single driving axle under the centre of gravity, for the purpose of equilibrating the entire weight of the engine, there remains but two other positions, viz . behind and close before the fire-box.

To illustrate the effect in both cases, let us suppose two engines, A and B, each of twelve tons weight in running order, with cylinders, boilers, and driving wheels of the same dimensions, and performing the same amount of duty, on two roads of exactly the same kind.

In the engine A, with the driving axle behind the fire-box, it was found that only half of its weight was brought into action for the purpose of producing friction, amounting in this case to $\frac{12}{2} = 6$ tons.

In the engine B, with the driving axle before the fire-box, two-thirds were found available for the same purpose, equal to $\frac{2 \times 12}{3} = 8$ tons. The ratio of adhesion is, therefore A : B = 6 : 8, meaning that the engine B possesses a surplus of two tons in its adhesive power, and, consequently, in its capability of drawing loads.

In further examining our subject another question arises, concerning the effect of the given ratio of adhesion on the rails. In the engine A, we have, as mentioned, six tons on the driving axle, and therefore, three tons on each driving wheel. In the engine B, however, we find eight tons on the driving axle, and, consequently, four tons on each driving wheel. The proportion of weight on the rails is accordingly, A : B = 3 : 4.

Supposing these two engines to run at the same speed, S and assuming the stress by impact upon the rails to be represented approximately by the speed multiplied into the weight imposed upon each driving wheel, then each line of rails would be percussed by A, with S x 3 = 3 S, and by B, with S x 4 = 4 S.

This gives a ratio of impact A : B = 3 S or A : B = 3 4 ; meaning, for the sake of practical illustration, that the engine B will ruin the rails, take them to be thirty-eight pounds per yard, after the lapse say of nine years; whilst the engine A, will produce the same deterioration only after the space of twelve years, supposing the amount of traffic and other conditions to be the same in both cases.

Although no actual observations of this nature have been made with regard to the rails, yet the average duration of the wrought iron tires on the driving wheels, proves the above proportion not to be an incorrect one. The duration of tires on engines, with the driving axle behind the fire-box, has been found to exceed the duration of those on engines with the driving axle before the fire-box; and taking the latter to be nine months at an average, the duration of the first has been found to amount to from twelve to fourteen months.

Wrought iron rails being manufactured in the same way as tires, it can be but a fair assumption, that the duration of rails will admit of the same proximate scale given in the above proportion of impact. This brief exposition, backed by the ratio of tractive power, A : B = 6 : 8, and by the proportion of duration, A : B = 3 : 4, makes it obvious why the diminution of impact in the engine B, possessing a superior power of traction was found of such great importance, and has thus constantly occupied the attention of the American ma-

THE LOCOMOTIVE ENGINE. 79

chinists and engineers. In pursuance of this notion, the eight wheeled engine was started with two driving axles, one before and the other behind the fire-box.

Supposing such an engine C to weigh twelve tons, in running order, and of the same dimensions as A and B, the weight on the two driving wheels was found to be also two-thirds, or eight tons, yet pressing upon the road on the four points of contact, only with $\frac{8}{4} = 2$ tons.

The proportion of adhesion or tractive power, is therefore, A : C = 6 : 8, B : C = 8 : 8, A : B : C = 6 : 8 : 8. The ratio of impact, or deterioration of the rails, being C : A = 2 : 3, C : B = 2 : 4, C : A : B = 2 : 3 : 4.

From this we may infer that rails lasting but nine years under the performance of the engine B, and twelve when traveled upon by engine A, will not meet with their ulterior destruction before eighteen years, when engines of the kind C are running upon them under the aforementioned suppositions.

I can, therefore, but applaud your resolution of building systematically, no other engine but those with eight wheels; four driving and four truck wheels. However, I feel myself called upon to impress you with the advantages that must necessarily result when the number of driving wheels can be augmented to six or eight, without losing that beautiful characteristic of the American engine, viz: the free vibrating truck, which in its office of piloting the engine along the track, I think invaluable for the American railroads, with their sharp turns and light superstructure.

An engine D, with three, and an engine E, with four driving axles, lending an opportunity to make their whole weight available for adhesion, which then would be that due to the maximum weight of twelve tons, in the given case, would certainly possess the greatest tractive power, and yet injure the road in a much less degree. The proportions of adhesion or tractive power, would be the following ones, supposing in every case that the engine possesses sufficient power to slip her wheels in pulling against a fixed point, A : B : C : D : E = 6 : 8 : 8 : 12 : 12; and the proportions of impact or deterioration of the rails, B : A : C : D : E = 4 : 3 : 2 : 2 : 1½. I am aware of all the difficulties attending what I propose, but I feel, nevertheless, confident that "flexible coupling rods," permitting all the axles, with the exception of the main driver, to conform to the radii of curves, are within the pale of practical feasibility. Only on this condition should I think myself justified in preferring engines with a greater number of driving axles than two, were I even inclined to overlook the greater complication that such a mechanical arrangement must require. I reckon simplicity to be one of the cardinal virtues in any mechanical apparatus, and of the most absolute necessity in the locomotive engine.

After this digression, permit me, gentlemen, to come back to the eight-wheeled engine, C, as the subject of my disquistion. Great as the improvement promised to be, in introducing the aforesaid engine, the advantages derived therefrom for the preservation of the rails, were however, nearly lost. The difficulty consisted in the stiff connection of the fire-box, boiler, smoke-box, and pedestals of the driving wheels with the frame, which acted like a lever. Whenever one pair of driving-wheels was raised by some irregular elevation in the track, resulting from its bad condition, the other pair, in consequence of the springs not acting quick enough to force them down, were momentarily lifted up by the frame, consequently without bearing their due proportion of weight; and on the contrary, when one pair was passing over a depression in the road, the other again, for the same reason had to sustain nearly the whole amount of weight originally allotted to both driving axles, the truck

THE LOCOMOTIVE ENGINE. 81

wheels always acting as a fulcrum, and the frame with its fixed pedestals and the axles therein revolving, as a lever.

This could not help injuring the road nearly in the same degree as the engine B; nay, the effects was still more injurious to the engine C itself, as in the case of the main driving axle being suspended by the frame in one of the aforesaid elevations, or depressions of the other driving axle, the former received its rotary motion from the pistons without its fulcrum, or adhesion to the rails.

It is but just to say, gentlemen, that you have saved the eight-wheeled engine from becoming a mere notion, and that owing to your exertions, it has been brought to such a state of perfection as ought to make the old six-wheeler of the kinds A and B, quite obsolete. It is furthermore but justice to state, that your special adaptation of the lever, or the balancing beam to the use of locomotives upon railways, obviated the aforesaid difficulties in such a manner as to leave but little to desire; and here I regret to say, that some of the northern railroads in Germany, notwithstanding the unqualified recommendation of so able an engineer as Mr. C. E. Detmold, have not adopted engines with your improvement.

I consider the balancing beam, supported in its centre by a vertical shaft, resting on springs that are attached by the pedestals to the frame, and stayed on its ends by two vertical pins abutting against the two driving axles, as possessing in an eminent degree the two indispensable qualities, first, of equalizing the weight on both driving axles, in whatever condition the road may be, and therefore, producing in an eight-wheeled engine of twelve tons a constant and equal adhesion of eight tons, yet pressing the rails with but two tons; and second, of furthermore diminishing the very ratio of impact as given above, the weight of the engine being suspended in the middle of the lever beam, causing it to fall only half the depth of any of the driving axles in their passage over any short or sudden depression in the track, while the engines A and B must go down the whole depth as supported by one axle alone, which by increasing the height of fall, must add to the power of the percussion, and therefore, ruin the road even in a shorter period than the proportionate number of twelve or nine years.

But this is not alone what distinguishes your engines; the balancing beam of your arrangement being now used by nearly all the engine builders of note in the United States, after having purchased the patent right from you, which at once bespeaks the great merit and usefulness of your improvement.

It is, besides, the very simplicity of your engines, that must engage the attention of even the least observing. Instead of four eccentrics, four eccentric rods, four latches, and a complicated arrangement to put them in and out of gear, by an extra hand lever, thus making three hand levers altogether—you have but two eccentrics, two eccentric rods, no latches, and a simple arrangement of the reversing valve; the whole to be handled by one and the same lever, and this too, by moving it in exact accordance with the required movement of the engine.

It is true that in reversing you lose in speed, as the lead of the slide no longer takes place; but this loss I think of no moment, as it only happens when the engine is backing. Besides the position of your forcing pumps is such as to prevent the freezing of the water, an advantage of great importance with locomotion in northern climes.

Gentlemen, this is my candid opinion about your eight-wheeled engines, and you are welcome to make any use of this document. Permit me to avail myself of this opportunity, to thank you for your readiness, and the frank and open way in which you satisfied my desire for information; and allow me to assure you that the modest and unostentatious manner in which you spoke of your engines,—trusting more to their own merits than to puffing and boisterous recommendations—has most favorably impressed me with your own personal character.

I am, gentlemen,

Yours, respectfully,

(Signed.) CHARLES MŒRING,
*Captain of Engineers in the Austr'an Army,
No. 342 Chestnut Street.*

Philadelphia, September 1st, 1840

[Reprinted from "Journal of Franklin Institute" for March, 1842].

Philadelphia, February 12, 1842.

MESSRS. BALDWIN & VAIL:

Gentlemen.—I send you inclosed, a statement of the performance of your new six-wheeled, geared engine, which you will perceive is in every way satisfactory. The train weighed 108½ tons, of 2,240 lbs., more than that hauled by your "Hitchens and Harrison" engine in February last, on our road.*

Statement of the performance of a six wheeled-engine, built by Messrs. BALDWIN & VAIL, *on the Philadelphia, Reading and Pottsville Railroad, February* 12, 1842.

This engine has six wheels and outside connections. The large drivers (forty-four inches in diameter), are behind the fire-box, and connected with the four truck wheels, (thirty-three inches in diameter), by cog gearing, in such a way as to obtain the adhesion of the whole weight of the engine, with little additional friction, and at the same time allow the requisite play in curves.

Her weight, in running order, is 30,000 lbs.; on her large drivers, 11,775 lbs.; or, 5,887 lbs. on each. On the truck wheel, 18,225 lbs.; or, 4,565 lbs. on each, and her cylinders are thirteen inches diameter and sixteen inches stroke.

This engine hauled, on the above date, a train of 117 loaded cars, weighing in all 590 tons, from Reading to the inclined plane, on the Columbia Railroad, fifty-four miles, in five hours and twenty-two minutes, being at the rate of over ten miles per hour the whole way.

*See the number of this Journal for May, 1841, page 319.

She consumed $2\frac{6}{10}$ cords of wood, and evaporated 3,110 gallons of water, with the above train. Weight of freight, 375 tons, of 2,240 lbs.; consisting of 259 tons of coal, twenty-two tons of iron and nails, and ninety-four tons of sundry other merchandise, including fifty-three live hogs, ten hhds. of whiskey, 188 bbls. flour, ship stuff, butter, &c. Weight of cars, 215 tons, making a total weight, not including engine and tender, of 590 tons of 2,240 lbs.

Whole length of train, 1,402 feet, or eighty-two feet over a quarter of a mile. The above train was transported in the ordinary freight business of the road, and was run without any previous preparation of engines, cars or fuel for the performance. The engine was closely watched at all the starts of the train, and not the least slipping of any of her wheels could be perceived. She worked remarkably well throughout the trip, turning curves of 819 feet radius, with ease to her machinery, and no perceptible increase of friction in her gearing. Her speed with the train on a level, was found to be nine miles per hour.

Whole length of level, over which the above train was hauled, twenty-eight miles; longest continuous level, $8\frac{1}{10}$ miles; total fall, from the point where the train was started to where it stopped, 210 feet.

The above train is unprecedented in length and weight, in Europe or America.*

G. A. NICOLS,
Superintendent of transportation on the Philadelphia, Reading and Pottsville Railroad.

U. S. GAZETTE, Feb. 14th.

---

*See Appendix, page 73, performance of Locomotive "Gowan & Marx" on same road, February 20th, 1840.

SIXTY HORSE POWER HARRISON BOILER.

HARRISON BOILERWORKS.

FIRE BRICK.
RED BRICK.

AN ESSAY

ON THE

STEAM-BOILER.

READ BEFORE THE

FRANKLIN INSTITUTE, PHILADELPHIA,

By JOSEPH HARRISON, Jr.,

MECHANICAL ENGINEER.

TO WHICH IS ADDED

A REPORT OF THE COMMITTEE ON SCIENCE AND ARTS, CONSTITUTED BY THE FRANKLIN INSTITUTE, ON THE

HARRISON STEAM-BOILER,

Etc., Etc.

REVISED EDITION.

PHILADELPHIA:
JAS. B. RODGERS CO. PRINTERS, 52 & 54 NORTH SIXTH STREET.
1873.

PREFACE.

Seven years' service in some of the largest establishments in New England and elsewhere, with boilers varying from Fifty to Fifteen Hundred Horse Power, with repeated orders from the same parties, shows that the " HARRISON " improved generator has taken a permanent place in the use of steam.

This boiler was first put in use at MESSRS. WILLIAM SELLERS & Co.'s works, in Philadelphia, in 1859. Its active manufacture commercially commenced in 1864; since which time more than 50,000 horse power of these boilers, have been made and put in use. Nearly six thousand horse-power were made in 1871, and a like amount will be nearly reached this year.

The above shows that it has fairly stood the test of many years of trial, and notwithstanding it has had to contend with a large share of prejudice, as well as interested opposition, its reputation at this time, is better than at any previous period.

I have the means of knowing just how much this large number of boilers have cost for repairs and maintenance, as all repairs and renewal to them emanate from these works, and I confidently challenge in this respect, a comparison with any other plan of boiler. I believe that the HARRISON BOILER, with the same care and attention, can be maintained safely, effectively, and economically, for any length of time at *one-half* less cost than any boiler now in use. (*See Page* 28.)

JOSEPH HARRISON, JR.

Harrison Boiler Works, Philadelphia.

December, 1872.

"*All boilers should be so constructed that their explosions may not be dangerous.*"

DR. ALBAN,
Of Plau in Mechlenburgh.

"Corrosion corresponds, in its comparative frequency and fatality, to the great destroyer of human life, consumption. It is the one great disease."

ZERAH COLBURN,
Before British Association at Bath, 1864.

"Furrowing along a seam of rivets, or rather the line of an over-lap, is found to be the usual malady." "So far as furrowing is concerned, there can be no doubt that *wrought-iron is the worst material* that can be employed for a steam-boiler."—*Report of Manchester and Midland Boiler Association, for* 1863.

"*Steam-boilers can no more be made absolutely secure against some kind of explosion or fracture than guns or ordinance.* But they should be, and can be made, so that no serious harm can arise when they do give way. To accomplish this most important end, the prevailing system has been found, after a century of trial, entirely at fault, and improvements must be looked for in its abandonment."—*Public Ledger,* June 14th, 1867.

A verdict of the Coroner's jury, in the case of an explosion at an Iron Works in Kensington, April 27th, 1868, signed by some of the first experts in Philadelphia, says:—

First. "That the defect that occasioned the accident was not apparent, nor could it have been detected until the small leak occurred on the morning of the 27th of April."

Second. "That the immediate detection of the defect, and the prompt attention given to it, shows that care and the *intention of safe working*, on the part of the engineer and managing partner, had been given in this instance, and that the *error of judgment* which allowed the use of the boiler after it had shown its defective condition, was one which the jury deplore—*they cannot blame* those who committed it." This "intention of safe working," and this "error of judgment," caused the loss, eventually, of six valuable lives.

AN ESSAY

ON

THE STEAM BOILER.*

AMONG the elements that have been pressed into man's service, water turned into steam holds a most important place. And strange as it may appear to the uninformed, it might almost be said, that the steam-engine, as matured by James Watt, came from his hands nearly perfect in principle,—armed and ready to do battle, in the varied fields in which it has since been employed. James Watt knew all, and acted with a knowledge of all, or nearly all, the principles that are now known. Improvements in the steam-engine of our time, consist in a better arrangement and proportion of parts, better material, better workmanship, and vastly increased size. Many of its better qualities are the result of improved means of manufacture, which with equally improved quality of material, has enabled the steam-engine builder to do such work as could not have been done under a less improved system, and for which Watt might have sighed in vain.

Not so the steam-boiler. It, from the very first application of steam as a useful agent, has been the constant trouble of the engine-builder and the engine user, the great source of anxiety, danger and expense. The first patent regularly issued in England for a steam-boiler, dates about a century back, and from that time to this, patents for new designs or improvements, numbering thousands, have been issued in the United States,—in England, and on the continent of Europe. Notwithstanding the vast amount of labor and thought that has been bestowed upon the subject, the whole engineering profession still is in doubt as to which is the best steam-boiler, no single one, at this

---

* Read before the Franklin Institute, January 16th, 1867, by Joseph Harrison, Jr., Philadelphia. (Revised and in part re-written.)

moment, proving so much better than the legion that surrounds it, as to take any very prominent place in the general estimation, and not one combining the most important principle of security against destructive explosion.

Stone, wood, cast and wrought iron, copper, steel and various alloys of other metals, have been tortured, bent and twisted, from the beginning, into almost every conceivable form to make a steam-boiler. Still the work of change goes on, patent upon patent being continually issued for attempted improvements in this much needed object. It is remarkable that changes have tended more towards saving weight, cost or fuel, than in the more important object of making it safe from explosion.

The paramount aim in the use of steam, should be safety, and yet, with all that has been done, no steam-boiler now in general use *approaches* this essential requisite in its construction, compared with what is demanded of it. Hence the frightful loss of life—the dreadful maiming and suffering, the immense amount of valuable property annually destroyed by steam-boiler explosions.

It may be said that there is no remedy for this state of things,— that all has been done that skill and ingenuity can devise, to stop such fearful results. If we *have* arrived at the end, and found no remedy, then must we accept the situation, trusting rather to Providence, care or chance, to protect us from harm, than to any inherent controlling principle in the thing used, voting steam a good servant but a very bad master.

Before concluding this paper, I will endeavor to show that all has not been done in the general use of steam, to render it as safe an agent, as its wide-spread utility and necessity demand. Nay, more; it will be shown, from many years of practical experience in the use of a steam-boiler of singular design, and of material not heretofore considered best for the purpose, that the employment of steam at any practicably useful pressure, *can* be made, almost entirely harmless.

Some writers give to Dr. Alban, of Plau, in Mecklenburg, the credit of first enunciating the grand idea that "*all boilers should be so constructed that their explosions may not be dangerous;*" but it is scarcely possible that Evans, Hancock, Gurney and others at a much earlier date, should not have as fully appreciated this most important principle.

When the low-pressure of the earlier era of the steam-engine was used, the form or material of the steam-boiler mattered little, and we find Savery using cast-iron, Newcomen wrought iron; but from the difficulty of getting good plates of the latter material, Watt even made and put in use boilers of *wood*, hooped in the manner of the soap-boiler's kettle, with cast iron curb at the bottom. But when the first really high-pressure engine was introduced by our countryman, Oliver Evans, carrying steam as high as *one hundred pounds to the square inch*, and upwards, it then became necessary to look for material and form capable of sustaining such pressure. Oliver Evans used wrought iron plates in plain cylinders of small diameters, sometimes, with internal return flue, through which the heated products of combustion passed, after coursing the whole length of the lower half of the boiler.

These two kinds of boiler are at this day more extensively used in the United States than any other, and may be found almost exclusively on our Western river steamers. Perhaps no other boiler now in such general use, has greater safety in its principle of construction than this of Oliver Evans.

It is true that the most disastrous explosions on record have occurred with cylinder boilers on our Western rivers, but these calamities have been the result of scanty proportions in the first place, in order to save cost and weight, or from depreciation after long use, rather than from defect in principle. If the grand idea insisted upon by Dr. Alban be the true one, then have our engine-builders wandered far away from it since the days of Oliver Evans. Look at the immense structures built up of wrought iron, now so largely made for, and used on ocean and river steamers! Is this principle of safety attained, or even aimed at, in these boilers? Are they so made that "*explosions are not dangerous?*" Witness the disaster on the North River steamer *St. John*, in 1865. Here a boiler exploded, made on an approved and often used plan, which, according to the testimony of experts on the Coroner's jury, "*pulsated*" at every stroke of the engine. Has any one seriously considered what this "*pulsating*" means? If anything, it means a movement in certain parts which, being kept up for a given and almost calculable length of time, must inevitably destroy the structure of the material of which these parts are made. It is not very assuring to the traveling public, that all of the best ocean steamers, as well as those on our rivers, lakes and sounds, have at this moment, boilers theoretically, if not actually, as unsafe as the one that blew up in the *St. John*. It is not too much to say, that all boilers of large dimensions, whether of square form, dependent upon stays or braces for their strength, or cylinders of large diameter, with or without internal flues, cannot be safe. Neither is it too much to say, that no boiler is safe, that can, under any circumstances, *rend and scatter large masses of material, liberating at the same time large volumes of highly charged water and steam.*

Take a boiler, if you please, that depends entirely for its strength upon being properly stayed, and there are thousands of such in use, especially for marine purposes. In the nature of boiler-work under such a system of construction, with the very best skill and the very best oversight, it is impossible to execute the work so as to be invariably reliable. Unlike almost every other class of work, even after the parts are finished, no matter how close the inspection, it is not possible always to know whether it has been well done or not. Let any one, with a full knowledge of the subject, watch the making of such a boiler. The drawings are perfect, every strain calculated to a decimal, every proportion exact. If it were possible to execute the work just as laid down, all might be well; but if such a thing is possible, we have never seen boiler-work made with such accuracy. In the matter of the stays (a most important point), every hole should be exactly smooth and true, and made to come in true line with the one it has to meet. Every bolt should be turned and fitted to its appropriate hole. But all who are acquainted with boiler-work, know that it is not even attempted to do it in this manner. Ill-shaped stays, badly made and badly fitted, or strained into ill-shaped places, often out of reach of the eye and the hand of the workmen;—rough holes most frequently made in the smith's shop, with as roughly made bolts. If the holes are bored, so rudely do they usually adjust themselves to one another, that the ever-ready drift—that bane of safe and good boiler-work—is resorted to, bringing the work together under a tension that puts to flight all decimal calculations, and but too frequently dismembers the parts themselves. Can such a boiler, dependent upon such work, be safe? A boiler, when finished, may be submitted to a water-pressure test; but this must not be too much relied upon, as this very test may so strain a steam-boiler, that a much less steam-pressure when fired, might lead to disaster.

And again, take plate-riveting. An English writer says:

"It is a truism, 'that the strength of any structure is its weakest point; but who can say where the weakest point of a steam-boiler is, as ordinarily made?'" "Take a simple cylinder boiler, for instance,— the sheets are run through the rolls and bent to the proper radius, and when the riveting gang get to work they close up the rivets with great rapidity; but when the holes come out of line with each other, the drift-pin is resorted to, and the sheets are literally stretched until the rivets can be inserted; when the drift-pin is knocked out, the sheet goes back to its place, and there is already, without a pound of steam-pressure, strain enough to cut the rivets off." "Repeat this performance through twenty or thirty feet, the length of an ordinary cylinder boiler, and who can say where the weakest point of the structure is? Suppose such a boiler made of silk or any flexible material, what shape would it be in?" "It would be full of puckers, folds, seams and gathers, and represent most accurately the various trials to which that most abused of all modern engineering apparatus—the boiler—is exposed." "The case is aggravated, not benefited, when we construct a square boiler, for this shape seems, by general consent, to have been adopted for marine service."

"When the angles or flanges of the sheets are not broken by the flange-turners, they are cracked out by the drift-pin of the riveting gang, and it ought to be made a capital offence to have such a tool on the premises of any boiler-works." "New boilers burst under the most mysterious circumstances; old boilers are patched and then burst; and we are told that 'putting new cloth into old garments is the solution of the trouble.'" "On each occasion the Coroner examines a host of 'experts,' who proceed to declare that the 'iron was burnt,'—'the water low,'—'the stays insufficient,'—'the water changed into explosive gases,' etc.; but it never occurs to these worthies, that the actual strength of the boiler was, in many cases, unknown, and that it may have been at the bursting point for many days, weeks, or months, until at length it gave way." "It is ridiculous to suppose that safety is secured by neat-looking rivet-heads or handsomely caulked seams." "Holes will come out of truth with the utmost care, especially in such hap-hazard work as punching." "Neither are the braces (stays) properly set; for some draw all one way, while others do not draw or hold at all, and are perfectly loose. Thus a portion do all the work, and the rest are idle;—they impart no strength, and are an element of weakness; for the engineer relies upon them when they are doing no good." "We are confident that a great deal of attention can profitably be given to the mere workmanship of steam-boilers;—they are not tanks for boiling water, but great magazines wherein tremendous power is stored, the safe custody of which is of paramount importance to all in the vicinity."

Assuming that a boiler of large dimensions, whether cylinder or marine, *can* be made so that all the parts are joined together without strain, this state of things can only exist at the uniform temperature throughout, under which the boiler has been made. Put fires at white heat into or under such a boiler, heating the plates in the immediate vicinity of the fire, as must occur, in a much greater degree than at the external or more remote parts of the structure: surely then the parts that had previously lain quietly together, assume a new and constantly changing condition, and who can tell what these changes are, their frequency, or to what extent the strength of the boiler is impaired thereby?

Let us now turn our attention to another equally, or perhaps more, important point than those we have been considering,—the wear and tear of plate-iron boilers. A writer in the *London Mechanics' Magazine* says: "It is not too much to say, that nine out of ten explosions are directly the result of corrosion." "Setting aside the value of human life and limb, we find that the mere pecuniary interests involved in either the gradual or sudden destruction of a boiler, are very considerable." "Repairs are, at all times, expensive, and the time lost in making them is often a serious source of pecuniary loss, worry and trouble." "Hence the replacement of a plate, or the alteration in a defective flue, is often staved off from day to day, until irreparable mischief is done." "Reflecting upon these things, it seems strange that boilers are made, fired and worked with a negligence, which apparently regards iron plates as indestructible, and the results of an explosion trifling to a degree." "We cannot set such a system, or rather such a want of system, down wholly to stupidity or neglect." "We know that boilers in the best hands, and under the most careful management, often become worthless with a startling rapidity, which no amount of theoretical reasoning can account for, nor practical skill arrest or delay." "The utter uncertainty in which the engineer is doomed to live, as to what does or does not promote durability, leads naturally to recklessness, neither the result of the want of thought nor indolence." "Corrosion is too often regarded in the light of a fate— a destroyer, merciless and indiscriminate, before which, as a *fetish*, the manufacturer and ship-owner bow down and submit."

Mr. Colburn, in a paper read before the British Association, in 1864, says: "As a boiler malady, corrosion corresponds in its comparative frequency and fatality to the great destroyer of human life, consumption. It is the one great disease." "A trickling of condensed steam down the outside of a boiler will inevitably produce corrosion, and to this was directly traced a large number of the forty-seven boiler explosions which occurred in the United Kingdom in 1863, and which caused the loss of seventy-six lives, with injuries, more or less serious, to eighty persons."

In the report of the Manchester and Midland Boiler Association, for 1863, we find the following: "Furrowing along a seam of rivets, or rather under the line of an overlap, is found to be the usual malady, but the iron is eaten away almost everywhere; not uniformly over the whole surface, but in numberless holes." "So far as furrowing is concerned, there can be no doubt that wrought iron is the *worst* material that can be employed for a steam-boiler."

Thus much on the subject of corrosion. Another article in the *London Mechanics' Magazine* says: "Until a comparatively recent date, the belief obtained with most engineers, that a riveted joint, if the work were properly done, was superior to the plate itself."

Mr. Wm. Fairbairn, in a series of carefully conducted experiments, upset this fallacy by proving, that, "the strength of the plate being taken as one hundred, that of a double-riveted joint will be seventy, and a single-riveted joint fifty-six;" and this with first-rate workmanship. "Fifty-six per cent. of the whole strength of boiler-plates is certainly not much to realize with the best workmanship; but as many boilers are put together, this percentage must be regarded as too high." "There are difficulties involved in the nature of the process, which the best mechanic can only combat—seldom or never overcome." "However accurately two plates may correspond before being punched, that process inevitably distorts them, and occasions a bad fit when subsequently put together." "The hammering and bending at the edges is invariably injurious to cold plates."

"Again, the best workmen, with the best machinery, find it out of the question to make all the holes in a long seam correspond." "The constant use of the drift is certain to follow, and when plates are of inferior quality or very thin, cracks are frequently established from one hole to the other."

"The judicious use of the caulking chisel easily conceals the defect, which is none the less serious because it is invisible." "The best rivets too seldom completely fill the holes they occupy." "They are never truly at right-angles to the plates, and are often exposed to enormous strain in drawing plates together when they are badly fitted." "We have seen, from this cause, the heads fly off half a score of '*Best, Best*' rivets at once, in rolling a new boiler from one side of the shed to the other."

Blistering of plates is another trouble in the use of plate iron. *Engineering Facts and Figures*, for 1863, page 21, says: "The fact of plates by good makers being liable to blister unawares, and which previous examination fails to detect, shows the importance of not hazarding an expression upon their soundness. Thus the strength of no unassisted plate, exposed to the action of the fire, should be relied on, and consequently it becomes most desirable that furnaces should be in every instance stayed either with flanged seams, or with hoops of angle iron, T-iron or other advantageous form."

Thus at every turn, the boiler-maker, in using wrought iron, meets with difficulties which can only be partially, never perfectly, overcome. These difficulties occur most frequently at the very points in the structure where danger from defective work or material is most imminent, and where it is least easy to avoid it.

The maintenance of a well-made steam-engine is of slight importance. So true is this, that engines are doing good service now in England, that were made by Watt and his contemporaries, the sun and planet-wheel even yet making their regular revolutions. Where are the boilers that started with these engines? Gone, gone, and many succeeding the first gone also.

The elements that destroy a steam-boiler commence their work from the moment of its completion, and from the hour it is first filled with water and fired. Whether used or not, the insidious process goes on, and it is fortunate if the life of the boiler reaches a decade, ere it is thrown out as worthless. From *Engineering Facts and Figures*, for 1865, we quote the following:

"The saying of that distinguished authority in matters mechanical, —Wm. Fairbairn,—'that danger in the use of high-pressure does not consist in the intensity of the pressure to which the steam is to be raised, but in the character and construction of the vessel which contains the dangerous element,' may be set down as a truism, containing a great deal of suggestive truth, but which is often overlooked, if not entirely ignored."

"Else how is the public sense of what ought to be, but unfortunately is not, every now and then shocked by a recurrence of those accidents which result in such extensive loss of life and property." "It is the saying of one who has said many good things in his day, that 'self-interest is always intelligent.'"

"In the matter of the use of boilers notoriously defective in form, material and construction, self-interest is *not* always intelligent; for

ESSAY ON THE STEAM BOILER. 13

however easily employers may take the loss of life from accidents in the use of steam-boilers, one would think that self-interest would prompt them to avoid, by all means in their power, the loss of property."

What are the conclusions that are forced upon us by all that has been adduced? Plainly that wrought iron has proved itself unfit for steam-boilers; that it is unreliable and unsafe to use it for such purpose, and that neither in principle nor workmanship, in the use of this material, have we advanced one step, in a century, towards making the steam-boiler, as now generally used, safe from destructive explosion. On the contrary, just in proportion as we have increased the working pressure, so have we run into greater danger; and at this moment boiler explosions are more frequent, and more fatal in their consequences, than ever.

It is a sad condition of things that this much needed force, should be so little within control. Must these mines of destruction, placed in our cities and towns, under our feet as we tread the sidewalk, and all around us, still hold their pent-up wrath by so frail a thread? Is there no way to render them more safe?* I think there is a way to do

---

* On September 9th, 1867, an explosion occurred in West Twenty-eighth Street, New York, in which a steam-boiler, weighing, as stated at the time, nearly five tons, was projected high in the air, and descending at a distance, horizontally, of not less than four hundred feet from the place it had previously occupied, crushed its way through, and almost destroyed, a large dwelling-house in its course. It may be stated that the establishment in which this boiler was used, became, at the first instant of the disaster, almost a complete wreck, killing and burying two of the workmen in its ruins. Its sudden and fatal effect in the home of innocent and unsuspecting childhood, is thus described in the New York *Times* of September 10th, 1867:

"A visit to the dwelling of Mr. Hausman, disclosed another scene of destruction. The flying boiler struck fairly upon the roof, a few inches from the rear wall, with the upper and smaller end descending. So great was the force of the descent of the huge mass, that the rear of the building crumbled and gave way beneath the descending weight of iron, which crushed through all of the four floors, and finally landed in the cellar. At the time of the explosion, one of the female servants employed by Mr. Hausman, named Mary Dowling, was on the attic floor in the rear, and immediately below her, on the third floor, were Maria Weiberzahl, the wet-nurse, and the infant, Henry Hausman, aged eleven weeks. The child had just fallen asleep, and the nurse had placed him in the crib while she began dressing herself. In the bath room, adjoining the nursery, was another child, Dora Hausman, aged nine years, who was bathing. The descending boiler fell on this portion of the building, and enveloped all four of these persons in the *debris*, the two children being instantly killed, the wet-nurse being severely injured, and the domestic, Mary Dowling, sustaining fatal injuries."

ESSAY ON THE STEAM BOILER.

this. If this can be shown, then let no one say hereafter that steam-boiler explosions cannot be prevented.

Mr. Wm. Fairbairn, whom we again quote, says: "Instead of working two hundred pounds pressure to the square inch, I think we shall reach five hundred pounds."

In *Engineering Facts and Figures*, for 1863, in treating of the great need of improvement in marine boilers, we find the following: "The answer is obvious,—no further economy can be obtained in steam-power without the use of *high-pressure* and expansion."

Ocean steamers, twenty-five years ago, used three or four pounds pressure to the square inch. Now the Cunard steamers use twelve or fifteen.

Our North River and Sound steamers, the pioneers in using much higher pressure in condensing engines, carry thirty or forty, and even fifty pounds to the square inch. Common consent, if not necessity, demands higher pressure, and it behooves the engineering profession to look to it, that we do not continue the present imperfect and most dangerous system, if there is any way to avoid it. Enough, we think, has been said to convince the most prejudiced that *a safe steam-boiler has not yet been made of wrought iron*. Assuming this to be proved, in what direction must we then look to find a better material for the purpose,—one, not possessing the defects of wrought iron,—one, that can readily be made into such forms as will most conduce to the safety, durability and economy of a steam-boiler?

Turn we now to cast iron,—early used, but heretofore and even now generally supposed inferior material for steam-boilers. A writer in the *London Mechanics' Magazine*, for May 2d, 1864, uses the following language:

"There is a French proverb which says, that we always return to our first love, and it is by no means unlikely that this will be verified in boiler engineering. At one period, it is beyond question that cast iron boilers were habitually used for very high pressures, and they were used because the material possessed constructive advantages which were not then believed to reside in wrought iron; and if these advantages reside in it still, under a principle of construction modified to meet existing demands, there is no good reason why it should not be habitually employed. Cast iron is far better adapted to meet the ordeal of fire and water to which a boiler is exposed, than the best wrought iron plates ever manufactured."

"As to strength, we all know, or ought to know, that that is a matter of proportion quite as much as a matter of material. There is nothing like practical illustration to bring such truths home to the mind. Let us suppose, then the case of two boilers, one made of plates half an inch thick, and the other one quarter of an inch thick. If each of these boilers is, say, six feet in diameter, the first one will possess, as nearly as may be, double the strength of the other. To render both of equal strength, it is only necessary to reduce the diameter of the thinnest one to half the diameter of the thickest."

"In the same way, it is certain that a cast iron tube, of a given diameter, may be made quite as strong as one of wrought iron of the same thickness, provided the diameters are proportioned, the one to the other, in the ratio of their tensile strength. That the arguments adduced against the use of cast iron are many and powerful, we do not pretend to deny; but that they are invariably applicable, or that it is, in other words, impossible to devise a boiler that shall elude these objections, is false."

"We daily see cast iron used to carry enormous pressures with the utmost confidence. Its tensile strength may always be brought, in one sense, up to wrought iron by using enough of it. It has thus beaten wrought iron, in the form of guns, many times."

"There are two ways of increasing the strength of any vessel; the one in increasing the thickness, the other in reducing the diameter of the globe or cylinder to be tested. It is obvious that cast iron can only be used in small tubes or chambers, inasmuch as large vessels must necessarily be of such a thickness, that heat would pass through it very slowly indeed. But this fact in no way militates against the safety, economy or efficiency of a generator. Perhaps the present system of employing wrought iron boilers of colossal dimensions in our every-day practice, has been productive of more injury to life and property, than can be laid at the door of the engineer on any other ground."

In a leading article in the *Engineer*, for 1864, it is said: "It has been so long the custom to consider cast iron as a brittle material, hardly to be trusted under pressure, that it requires some amount of reflection to perceive wherein it possesses manifest advantages over wrought iron. The resisting strength of a properly made cast iron boiler is calculable, and a good *a priori* case could have been made out in its favor long ago."

In an article in the *American Artisan*, for November 22d, 1865, in answer to an assertion made in that journal, referring to the Harrison

Boiler, that "cast iron was not to be recommended for steam-boilers," because it "was liable to be strained from inequality of temperature," I have said, "Many years of experience in the use of this boiler has taught me that, as a material for steam-boilers, cast iron is preferable to wrought iron, and for a reason that can be easily understood. Cast iron is *not* LIABLE TO BE STRAINED 'by inequality of temperature;' *it is liable to break* from such cause, and will give out at once if badly proportioned or improperly used. Wrought iron in steam-boilers *is liable to be strained by* 'inequality of temperature,' and not fracturing at once, goes on straining until its structure is destroyed, and the parts thus strained inevitably give way."

"Put cast iron in such a form as will prevent harm in case of rupture, and it becomes the *best* material for steam-boilers, and one of its best qualities is in giving out when badly treated. Not so wrought iron, its very tenacity begetting a false security, which might lead to disaster at any moment."

It certainly appears strange at a first glance, that brittleness in any material should make it more reliable than a more tenacious one, for purposes needing strength.

In the finding of the Coroner's jury in a recent boiler explosion in the city of Philadelphia, by which five men lost their lives, we find the following:

"That those in charge of these boilers exhibited culpable negligence in regard to the precautions universally considered as essential to the safe management of steam-generators, and were not sufficiently experienced to render their management of such apparatus safe. A similar want of knowledge, experience and care is only too common among those using steam-power."

"That the proprietor was guilty of neglect in failing to provide a competent engineer to take charge of the steam motors of the establishment."

"In connection with this occurrence, this jury reiterates what has been already most strongly expressed under like circumstances, that official inspection of all steam-boilers should be provided by our local government, and is as essential to the safety of life and limb among our citizens as any part of our police regulations. The storage of gunpowder in our city is prohibited by law; but any one may place a steam-power magazine, with match burning, at our side or under our feet, with perfect impunity." "Such magazines undermine, in fact, our most crowded streets, and, unless properly cared for, will one day reveal their existence in terrible disaster."

ESSAY ON THE STEAM BOILER. 17

There is much for reflection in these extracts, and their teachings should not be passed unheeded. In the use of steam in stationary engines, of small size in our large cities and towns (and from these as much harm can arise as from larger ones), it is almost the rule to employ men of little experience or skill, who are utterly incompetent to fill the most important post of fireman.

The fact that they themselves are in the greatest danger, fails to make them more thoughtful, and they ignorantly and carelessly go on, from day to day, hanging on the very verge of disaster. Almost unaware of the tremendous power that is in their keeping, and failing to profit by the plainest evidences of danger, a long continued immunity often leads them recklessly to think that no harm can arise, even when danger is most imminent.

And in the matter of inspection of boilers of stationary steam-engines, insisted upon so strongly, something also may be said. It is no doubt true that the regular government inspection of steamboat boilers has been productive of good; but, at the same time, too much reliance should not be placed upon even this safeguard. It is well known that a steam-boiler may pass inspection, and be, at the moment, all right; but it is equally well known that even in an hour thereafter, it may, by neglect, become entirely unsafe.

A steam-boiler may pass the most critical examination, and may stand a severe hydraulic test when cold, but a much less pressure, superadded to the strains resulting from irregular expansion, when hot, might rend the same boiler into fragments.

It has been conceded "that the strength of any structure is its weakest point." Let us now consider how a parity of reasoning will apply to the use of steam. In almost every case of boiler explosions, we have the changes rung upon the stereotyped words, "culpable neglect in some essential particular," "gross ignorance," or "carelessness," and that closer and more frequent official inspection, greater skill and more careful oversight on the part of those in charge, would have prevented the catastrophe. So it might, in some instances, no doubt; but it should be borne in mind, that neglect and carelessness (whether wilful or not), as well as the most stupid ignorance, may always be counted upon.

Hence we should adopt as an axiom, that safety is to be looked for amidst the greatest amount of ignorance, or even wilful carelessness and neglect, with which steam-generating apparatus may be used, without causing disaster, rather than in the exercise of the greatest care and skill.

It is worth while to reproduce here in part a leading article from the *Public Ledger* of June 13th, 1867, just one week after the dreadful calamity in Sansom Street, Philadelphia, when nearly thirty persons were hurried into eternity, maiming many others, and utterly destroying a large manufactory in a moment of time:

"PREVENTION OF BOILER EXPLOSIONS.

"The recent steam-boiler explosion warns us again, in tones not soon to be forgotten, that greater security to life and property in the use of steam has become a paramount necessity; and, leaving out all other considerations, the subject demands the earnest attention of every one who values his own personal safety. The public will be again told that ignorance and want of experience,—reckless, if not wilful neglect of the most obvious precautions,—material and workmanship of bad quality,—low water,—over pressure,—explosive gases,—electricity, or some other such thing has been the cause of this terrible calamity. But it must not be overlooked that steam-boiler explosions, largely destructive to life and property, have occurred more than once in the largest, most experienced and most carefully managed engineering and manufacturing establishments in our city.

"And it must also be borne in mind that it is quite impossible to procure boiler-plates of wrought iron invariably reliable, or that will remain so, no matter how much care is bestowed upon their manufacture or inspection. It is equally certain that the best material ever put together with the very best workmanship, under the present system, may, and does frequently, share the same fate as the most inferior. Thus, whether these much used appliances are made as near perfection as may be, directed by intelligent and skillful management, or the reverse, their end is but too often the same. Under such a condition of things it is not worth while to waste time in theorizing as to questionable causes. It is with the disastrous results and their possible remedies, that wise men should deal.

"Steam-boilers can no more be absolutely secure against some kind of explosion or fracture, than guns or ordnance. But they should be and can be made so that no serious harm can arise when they do give way. To accomplish this most important end, the prevailing system has been found, after a century of trial, entirely at fault, and improvements must be looked for in its abandonment.

"Councils, if they have the power, or if they have not, then the State Legislature, in their efforts to enforce stringent rules for the inspection of all boilers of the kind that are known to be liable to disastrous explosions, should try the experiment of an ordinance or law, that no boilers, after a certain date, shall be erected within our city limits, unless a certificate is first obtained from competent inspectors, that an explosion of said boiler *will not be dangerous.* There is no full security in any direction, pass what law you will, make what inspection you may.

"The time is not far distant when the present system must come to an end, unless it can be proved beyond all doubt that no change for the better is possible. The public safety now demands that these engines of destruction shall no longer be kept hidden from sight in the basements of our most densely peopled neighborhoods, or in our crowded workshops, and even under the busy footways over which we unconsciously tread, always ready for havoc, and only perhaps temporarily held from repeating the horrors of last Thursday, by a constantly weakening chain, the real strength of which is seldom if ever known.

"If these destructive engines were new things, and it was now first proposed to place hundreds of them in our crowded thoroughfares and under our pavements, who would listen to such a proposition? It would not be entertained for a moment. Neither should the system itself, although it is well established, be tolerated for a day beyond the time when it can be dispensed with."

It is beyond controversy or doubt, that the fracture of steam-generating apparatus, can and may occur, under any system of construction. No amount of official inspection or special care can entirely prevent this, and it must be set down as an imperative law, if safety is to be secured, "*that all boilers should be so constructed that their explosions may not be dangerous.*"

Having said thus much upon the general question of steam-boilers, it now becomes my province to describe the

HARRISON STEAM-BOILER,

An invention of my own, now being largely made and rapidly introduced into practical use. I had long turned my attention to the subject of improving the steam-boiler, and believing that better guiding principles were needed, I at length fixed in my mind the following axioms:

1st. That a steam-generator of whatever form or material, must, as a paramount condition, be absolutely secure from *destructive explosions, even when carelessly used.*

2d. That it must be constructed upon a system or series of uniform parts, simple in form, few in number, easily made, and easily put together or taken apart, and not of costly material.

3d. That its strength should in no respect be dependent upon any system of stays or braces, whereby the inefficiency or rupture of one of these braces or stays could cause greatly increased strain upon the others, thus endangering the whole structure.

4th. That its parts should not be of great weight or size, thus permitting greater portability and greater facility for getting it into or out of place.

5th. That it must have a principle of renewal, allowing the easy displacement and replacement or interchange of any one or more of its parts, without disturbing or impairing the material or workmanship of the remaining portions of the structure.

6th. That a boiler, whether of large or small dimensions, should have uniformly such elements of strength, as would render it always capable of safely sustaining many times greater pressure, than need ever be demanded of it in practice, and that its safety should not be impaired by corrosion, or the many other harmful influences, which so soon and so seriously affect the strength of ordinary boilers.

7th. That the parts should be so made and put together, that in case of rupture of any portion of the boiler, no general break up of the structure could occur, the release of the pressure by such rupture merely causing a discharge of the contents, without explosion or serious disturbance of any kind.

8th. That it should be constructed so as to facilitate the certain removal of deposit from its interior or exterior surface.

These axioms being carried out, all else being equal, it is believed that the result must be a better and safer steam-generator than any that has preceded it. It is not important here to enter into the detail of how the "Harrison Boiler" reached its present form. Suffice it to say, that when the form of a hollow sphere and curved neck was decided upon, as shown in the illustrations herein, it seemed that the true principle had been arrived at—that nothing more could be desired in that direction.

HARRISON'S CAST IRON STEAM BOILER.
Detail of 4-Ball Unit.

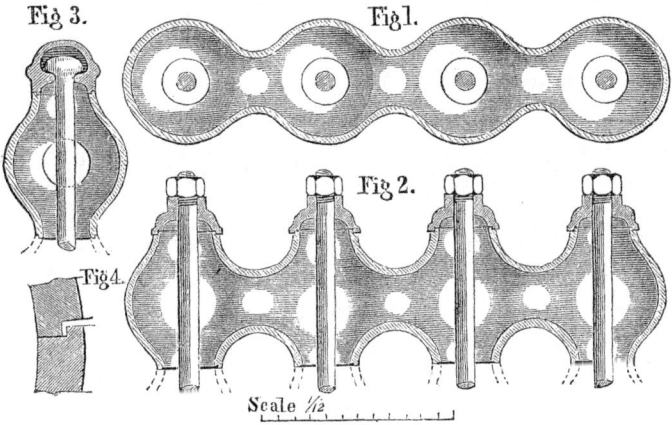

Fig. 1. Transverse Section. Fig. 3. Sectional Plan.
Fig. 2. Longitudinal Section. Fig. 4. Section of Joint. Half Size.

A boiler of about seventy-five horse-power, the first of the kind, was made of these simple elements, in the spring of 1859, and put in operation at the establishment of Messrs. Wm. Sellers & Co., Philadelphia.

This boiler effectively and economically supplied steam for driving the extensive workshops of the above firm, for several months. Its trial settled the question previously in doubt even with myself, that a boiler, as hereafter to be described, could be made and used, without its integrity being disturbed by irregularity of expansion and contraction consequent upon the action of fire.

In practice up to the present time, it has been usual to cast the spheres of eight inches in external diameter and scant three-eighths of an inch thick, placed in groups of two and four, making what may be called a brick and a half brick. These spheres are arranged in a straight line, one inch apart between their external diameters, and are connected with each other by a curved neck about three and one-quarter inches in diameter inside, at the smallest part. A series of half-necks make openings entirely through each of the spheres, at right-angles to the necks previously described.

These groups of spheres are called "units," and when jointed with a rebate-joint, accurately made on the edge or least diameter of the half-necks, fit closely together, making, when these edges are adjusted and drawn together, a steam and water-tight joint. Any number of these two and four sphere units, when placed together with break-joints, may be conveniently made into a parallelogram or other form that may be desired. The distance between the centres of the spheres in the direction of the jointed or half-necks, when the units are laid together, is the same as the distance in the transverse direction, thus making an uniform section of any given length or breadth. Wrought iron tie-bolts pass through each line of spheres in the direction of the half, or jointed necks, connecting at each end with caps that close up the external orifices of the section. One of the caps, called a blank cap, is made to receive a T-head at one end of each bolt; the other end of the bolt passing through the opposite cap, and ending outside with screw and nut.

It will be seen that these tie-bolts will bind all the units in one section firmly together.

A section of six spheres wide, the upper rows twelve, and the four lower rows thirteen spheres long, will make a boiler of about six horse-power.

In setting a boiler ordinarily for stationary purposes, one or more of the sections are placed on edge, at an angle of about forty degrees, side by side, usually one inch apart between the sections, the upper corner on the bottom line being supported on a cast iron rail or bearer, the lower portion resting on a chair, adapted to the purpose, placed behind the bridge wall. A common steam-pipe, taking steam from the upper caps, connects any number of sections together. A similar pipe, in like manner placed at the bottom corner of the section, makes a water-connection between any number of sections.

To avoid binding of the parts from irregular expansion or disturbance of any kind, the steam and water-pipes are made up of short pieces, joining with spherical joints, held together with tie bolts, after the manner of the units. By this means a flexible connection is made, that prevents all trouble in joining the sections together.

No attempt is made to provide steam room, other than the capacity of the spheres in the upper angle of the sections above the water-line.

It is found in ordinary practice with the largest boilers, using high-pressure steam through an engine, that the steam-room allowed as above is quite sufficient. A larger proportion may be required for low-pressure engines, or where steam is taken out at irregular intervals in large quantities, and this may be easily had by adding to the number of the upper units.

The heated products of combustion rise from the grate, passing

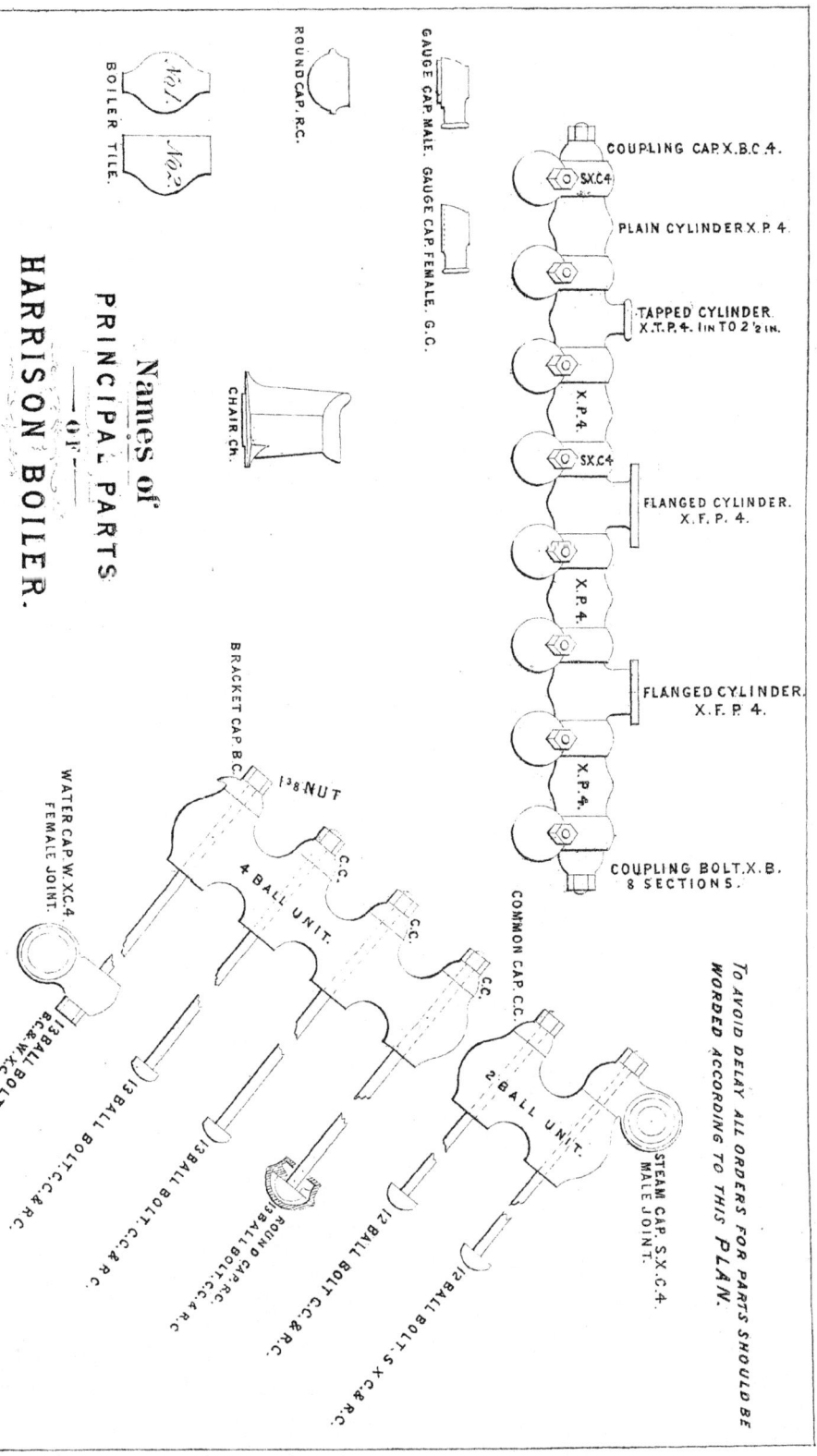

between the sections, and amongst the spheres, and over the bridge-wall, finding exit at length towards the chimney, at the lowest and coldest part of the boiler. A cast iron guard is inserted between each section, nearly horizontal, a short distance below the water-line. This guard prevents active heat from reaching the steam-spheres, but sufficient heat reaches the upper angle of the boiler, to dry and superheat the steam, ere it reaches the outlet to the steam-pipe at the upper cap.

It is not essential that a stationary boiler should be set exactly as described, as the units may be built up vertically, horizontally, or in any irregular manner best suited to the circumstances of the case. A stationary boiler set after the manner first indicated, and heretofore most generally adopted, has given very good and very economical results, when compared with other boilers having the best reputation.

MATERIAL OF BOILER.

Having, as I think, in the previous pages, fairly proved that cast iron may be preferred to wrought iron as a material for steam-boilers, let me say a few words in regard to the advantages of the former material as used in the "Harrison Boiler."

Mr. Zerah Colburn, late editor of the London *Engineer*, and now editor of the new magazine published in London, called *Engineering*, has written much and very ably on the steam-boiler. His opinion, therefore, is entitled to great respect.

In a paper on steam-boilers, read by him before the Institution of Mechanical Engineers, at Birmingham, on May 5th, 1864, in alluding to mine, he says:

"Although it cannot be said that cast iron is in itself a strong material for boilers, yet it will be seen that in the form now described, it affords greater absolute strength against bursting than is possessed by any form of plate iron boiler. In a 'unit' of four spheres, each sphere having an internal diameter of about seven and a quarter inches, the whole area of the plane in which a bursting pressure could act, taken through the eight openings of the four spheres, is two hundred and twenty square inches, whilst the least section of iron resisting this pressure in the same plane is twenty-seven and a half square inches. In tensile strength may be safely taken at five and a half tons to the square inch. At this rate the bursting strength of the units would be one thousand five hundred and forty pounds."

ESSAY ON THE STEAM BOILER.

And again, Mr. Colburn, in a paper read before the British Association for the Advancement of Science, at Bath, in 1864, says: "In ordinary boiler-making the geometrical advantage of the hollow sphere cannot be turned to account. It cannot be produced economically in plate iron, nor if in plate iron, could it be advantageously employed in a steam-boiler.

"The hollow sphere has this property, to wit: with a given thickness of metal it has twice the strength of a hollow cylinder of the same diameter. This is upon the assumption (which is correct when the cylinder is of a length greater than its own diameter) that the ends of the cylinder offer no resistance to a bursting pressure exerted against its circumference.

"Under over-pressure, a closed cylinder would take the shape of a barrel, and if of homogeneous material and structure, it would burst at the middle of its length in the direction of its circumference. The circumference of a sphere of a diameter of one, being 3.14159, the sum of the length of the two sides of a cylinder of the same diameter, and having a plane of rupture of the same area, is 1.5708, or exactly half as much."

And in the same paper, he says: "The tensile strength of cast iron varies between five tons and fifteen tons per square inch. Considered as a material for boilers, only the minimum strength should be regarded." "Cast iron boilers of eight feet in diameter, and of great length, were at one time made, but these were manifestly objectionable. The spherical form of a moderate diameter is preferable, and whatever is the strength of a riveted wrought iron cylinder, that of a cast iron sphere of the same diameter and same thickness of metal, will be the same.

"Plate iron of a strength of eighteen tons per square inch is virtually weakened to ten tons by the loss in riveting, and as the hollow sphere is twice stronger than the hollow cylinder of the same diameter and thickness, the cast iron having no joints, becomes equal in this comparison to the wrought plates."

"If we could always count upon the maximum strength of iron, to wit: twenty-seven tons per square inch for wrought and fifteen tons for cast, a fourteen feet cast iron sphere would have the same strength to resist bursting as the seven feet cylinder of the Lancashire forty-horse boiler, supposing the same thickness of metal in each case."

"But there is no occasion to make a boiler as a single large sphere; for it is now ascertained from extensive experience that hollow cast iron spheres of small diameter do not retain the solid matter deposited by the water. Small water-tubes, and indeed all small water-spaces in ordinary boilers, always choke with deposit when the feed-water contains lime; but cast iron boiler spheres, although they may be temporarily coated internally with scale, are found to part with this whenever they are emptied of water. *This fact is the most striking discovery that has been made in boiler engineering.*" It removes the fatal defect of small subdivided water-spaces, which can now be employed with the certainty of their remaining constantly clear of deposit.

"This discovery has been made in the use of the cast iron boiler invented by Mr. Harrison, of Philadelphia, United States."

"In Manchester, with feed-water taken from the Irwell, or from the canal, a hard scale is soon formed in the ordinary boilers; but in the cast iron boiler, a succession of thin scales of extreme hardness are found to form upon, and to become detached of themselves, from the inner surfaces of the water spheres. The scales are blown out with the water at the end of the week, and only small quantities can be found when purposely sought for. A pint of loose scales and dirt is the most that has yet been found in a careful internal examination, after nine months daily work." "None of *the cast iron is removed with the scale.*"

"The self-scaling action, which has been found to be the same in all cases where the boiler has been worked, can only be explained by conjectures, which it is not, perhaps, necessary to introduce in the present paper. It deserves the careful investigation of the chemist and mechanical philosopher, with whom the author prefers to leave the subject."

This property of casting the scale was not aimed at or expected, when the Harrison boiler was designed. It is true, nevertheless, that after three months trial of my first boiler, at Messrs. William Sellers & Co., in 1859, no scale or other deposit was found therein, all that had thus far been formed having been removed by blowing out once a week. Still, this short experience seemed hardly sufficient to establish a rule.

But, in addition to what has been stated by Mr. Colburn, a continued experience, running through many successive years, in Philadelphia and elsewhere, has proved that, as a general rule, the Harrison Boiler *does* regularly shed its scale by blowing it out, under certain directions, once a week, although this property should not be relied on to keep it clean.

There are, I think, several reasons why this peculiar form of steam-generator should have this property. In the first place, cast iron, as a material for steam-boilers, has not the same tendency towards continued oxydation as wrought iron.

I do not think that the hollow sphere, in itself, has any special quality for throwing off scale; still, I think it will be seen that the hollow sphere, in connection with the curved neck, may have this quality in some degree. If the form of the interior of one of the units of the Harrison Boiler is examined, it will be found that but little of its inside surface makes a complete arch or continuous ring.

A hollow sphere, without opening of any kind, would bind deposit to its inner surface, just as it is bound in a tube of equal diameter, and from which it is often so difficult to be removed. In almost every instance in the "units" of the Harrison Boiler, the reversed curved line comes in to break up the continuous ring, and removes the abutment of the arch.

The boiler should be blown off frequently during its working hours, when broken scale and organic matter is in suspension in the water. It should certainly be blown out entirely empty under pressure once a week, after the fires are drawn and the furnace walls cooled down to a moderate temperature. On no account should a boiler be emptied while the walls are red hot. In some instances, owing to the peculiar nature of the water, a *soft* or a very *hard* deposit may occur, that will not crack off or blow out as above. To avoid trouble from this cause, it is necessary that some of the lower bolts be taken out for examination, say once in three months. This *soft* or *hard* deposit being found, the boiler must be kept clean thereafter by taking out the bolts, and clearing the deposit with a scraper adapted to the purpose, or by the use of solvents.

Interior deposit, next to corrosion, is the great evil that most seriously affects all steam boilers, and it is not pretended that the Harrison Boiler is free from this trouble.

Many schemes are resorted to for removing interior deposit, and if the same amount of time, trouble and expense, were applied in preventing the introduction of injurious matter, the evils that arise would in a great degree be remedied.

The great problem in steam, has been its generation, its use being a comparatively easy matter. Yet we find engine builders give most attention to improvement in the making and managing of the engine, leaving usually that more important thing—the boiler—to take care of itself.

ESSAY ON THE STEAM BOILER. 27

Firemen or stokers, on whom rests every moment, very great responsibility, are but too often allowed to bungle along in their own ignorance and stupidity. If they can be taught to note the height of water, and to shovel coal into the furnace, this is about all that can be expected of them.

CIRCULATION OF WATER.

It is believed that the steam-boiler under consideration has many advantages in its water and steam circulation. When set, at an angle of about forty degrees, the currents of water, in each section, when generating steam, ascend along the line of spheres nearest the fire, and through the intersecting necks, carrying with these currents the accumulating steam, and delivering it at the upper angle, or steam-room portion of the section. The descending water-currents, at and near the water-level, find their way downward along the upper ranges of spheres, and through the intersecting necks, reaching at length the lower angle of the sections, from which point the circulation is continued, and goes on as before.

It should be noted that each section of this generator, no matter how large the whole structure may be, has in itself a separate and thorough system of water and steam circulation. In fact, each section is a distinct boiler.

FIRE CIRCULATION.

The boiler under consideration, it is believed, has several advantages in the application of heat thereto. Its peculiar form softens the lines of circulation for the heated products of combustion, leaving no abrupt turns or out-of-the-way corners, so often found in the more complicated boilers, and at the same time presenting a series of uniform channels, with their equally uniform surrounding surfaces, for taking up the heat. Unlike the long and narrow tube of the tubular boiler, each channel of fire circulation in this is in full connection with all the others, both vertically and laterally, causing a better blending of the elements that support combustion, and thus maintaining it for a longer period than can be done in the long narrow tube.

It has been proved by repeated experiment, that tube fire-surface (say in tubes of two inches external diameter and under) has a greatly reduced value, after the first two or three feet from the fire, when compared with fire-box surface.

In some carefully conducted experiments made under my notice at St. Petersburg, Russia, it was found, in boiling water in the open air, that copper tubes of two inches external diameter and one-tenth of an inch thick, laid horizontally, were very nearly equal to fire-box surface, in evaporating power, for a distance of two and a half feet from the fire. Beyond that distance their value fell off rapidly, and five feet, with a most intense fire, seemed the maximum of really valuable fire-surface. Between the ninth and tenth foot (the latter being the extreme length of the tubes,) water could not be raised to two hundred and twelve degrees, after hours of continuous firing.

These experiments were made with a fire-box twenty inches diameter, and twenty inches high, out of which proceeded, horizontally, four copper tubes of the dimensions above stated. Care was taken to ascertain the exact evaporating value of each separate foot of tube-service in the direction of their lengths, as well as the value of fire-box surface.

Flame, or inflammable vapor, entering a tube of small diameter, may, at the moment of entrance, be in full combustion, and have a temperature nearly equal to the source from whence it springs. Passing into a tube, one and eight-tenths inches internal diameter, surrounded by boiling water, the metal in the tube would have a temperature of not much above two hundred and twelve degrees. Vapor, with no addition to its supply of oxygen, coming in contact with this low temperature of the tube, would soon be reduced below the point of combustion, and from that moment, no matter what heat-giving properties it might still possess, they would be of no further effect, and to the end of the tube the vapor would give off heat only as heated air.

MAINTENANCE.

From the small size of the parts, and the ease with which they are put together or taken to pieces, it will be seen that injured parts of the Harrison Boiler can be renewed with great facility. A sphere may crack, or portions of the sections, nearest the fire, may, from neglect, become overheated and spoiled. The taking out of a few bolts permits the displacement of defective parts, without disturbing the uninjured portions; replacement, being equally convenient. When the heating surface is entirely worn out and rendered useless, it can be renewed and the boiler made as good as at first, for one-half of the original cost, of the whole boiler complete. The ordinary wrought iron boiler when worn out, is scarcely worth the cost of removal.

TRANSPORTATION.

The facility with which this boiler can be maintained, will explain why it is easy of transportation. Usually it is sent from the workshop in sections convenient and safe to handle, each weighing about a ton. These sections can be put into place, if necessary, through an opening five feet long and one foot wide.

If it is required to still further reduce the size of the separate parts, a section may be taken to pieces, so that no portion need weigh more than eighty pounds.

Thus a boiler, no matter what may be its ultimate size, can be carried in detail in a man's hand, and may, if necessary, be put through an opening one foot square. The hauling, transporting and placing of the unwieldy wrought-iron boiler is always a source of great expense,—often of danger.

Many a boiler has been run much nearer the point of disaster than it would otherwise have been, had its removal and replacement been a matter of more speedy and easy accomplishment. Many a disastrous explosion has occurred, and many a valuable life lost, for no better reason.

EXTERNAL CLEANING.

It is always difficult to keep the ordinary steam-boiler entirely free from soot and other deposit on its fire-surface, whether in flues, plain cylinders, or the other numerous forms in which it is made.

The fire-passages of the Harrison Boiler, being uniform, and all in connection with one another, external cleaning becomes a very simple process. A steam jet is best adapted to this purpose, and a convenient apparatus of this kind is attached to each boiler, so arranged that its use for a few moments every day, will keep the external surface of the spheres clean.

TENDENCY TO RUPTURE.

Steam at ordinary working pressure has little tendency to rupture any of the parts of this boiler. Neither has the steam pressure any great tendency to separate the joints, as the necks, being but three and one-quarter inches in inside diameter, might be held together, under a pressure of one hundred pounds per square inch, with a bolt no larger than would sustain a strain of about eight hundred and thirty pounds.

Allusion has been previously made to the evils that affect all boilers from irregular expansion when in use. It is equally necessary in the Harrison Boiler to guard against this influence.

It may be well here to consider this most important feature more fully.

The powerful and irresistible action of this force, begins its work at the moment fire is first applied to a steam-boiler, and little by little, too surely impairs its strength. It is most difficult to control when the material is in such form as not to admit of compensation or allowance, when subjected to its injurious effects.

In ordinary boilers made of wrought iron, it is practically impossible to arrange the parts so as to prevent irregular expansion, and consequent undue strain, from this cause. As it has been shown that it is equally impossible to make and put such boilers together when new, without undue strain, we have here two most powerful influences at work, tending to rend the parts asunder (entirely irrespective of steam-pressure), the importance of which as elements of danger, are seldom, if ever, taken into account.

Take a plain cylinder, if you please, the most simple form into which wrought iron can be put, to make a steam boiler: put a fire under such a boiler, expending its most intense heat upon a short portion of one-half of its lower diameter, at the end over the fire-grate, the products of combustion thereafter, coursing along the whole length of the remaining half diameter, until the outlet to the chimney is reached. Under these circumstances, the lower line must be very materially increased in length over the upper, and the whole structure will be then subjected to a series of complicated strains, the position and nature of which we can only conjecture, but cannot provide against. Extra thickness of material will not always remedy, and might aggravate the evil.

In more complicated boilers, this terrible ordeal is often yet further intensified. Make such boilers of brittle material,—putting them into shape, entirely free from strain (if this were possible), and let them be fired in the same manner as if made of wrought iron. That such boilers would break in pieces ere long is not doubtful. Made of wrought iron, they might not break up at once, but their greater tenacity would give them no immunity from the influences that had so soon destroyed their more brittle competitor, and which might in the end prove alike fatal to both. It is not a very hopeful view, when we consider that these undue strains are not lessened when the boiler becomes weakened by corrosion, or has its strength impaired by any other cause.

ESSAY ON THE STEAM BOILER. 31

Cast iron expands less at the same temperature than wrought iron, and this difference might seem likely to interfere with the tightness of the joints in the Harrison Boiler. But with the compensating curved lines of the units, and a due proportion being maintained between the bolts and the spheres, no trouble need arise from irregular expansion.

DURABILITY.

In an experience of many years with this boiler, no serious gradual depreciation has ever shown itself in any of its parts, and except from overheating or "*burning*," arising from low water or other causes, and consequent warping of the "units," which, of course, destroys the accuracy of the joints, it has not shown any decided marks of depreciation.

SECURITY FROM EXPLOSION.

By what has been adduced it must be seen that the Harrison Boiler is safe from destructive explosion. It is not, however, maintained that it cannot, under undue strain, be ruptured in some of its parts, or that it might not do injury, consequent upon a sudden discharge of water or steam. But it *is maintained*, that under no circumstances can it "*rend and scatter large masses of material, liberating at the same time large volumes of highly charged water and steam.*"

On page 131 of the *Journal of the Franklin Institute* for February, 1867, will be found a report of the "Committee on Science and the Arts" of the Franklin Institute, giving an account of certain severe tests that the Harrison Boiler was put to, in the effort to destroy it by steam-pressure and other means. The attempted destruction utterly failed. Attention is called to this report, at page 39, as exhibiting some very remarkable results.

When it is considered that eight hundred and seventy-five pounds per square inch of steam-pressure, failed to burst any of the spheres in one of the sections,—that under such severe test every joint becomes a safety-valve, and when it is certain that, under all circumstances, the general integrity of the whole structure can be surely maintained (a point most positively insisted upon), then but slight injury can arise, in any contingency.

CONCLUSION.

Considering the plan, material and mode of manufacture of the Harrison Boiler, let us now revert to the *axioms* laid down as guiding principles in making a steam-boiler, and see how far they have been carried out.

1st. The boiler under consideration *is theoretically and practically safe from all destructive explosion, even when carelessly used.*

2d. *It is constructed upon a system or series of uniform parts, few in number, easily made, and easily put together or taken apart, and not of costly material.*

3d. *Its strength is in no respect dependent upon any system of stays or braces, whereby the inefficiency or rupture of one of these braces or stays can cause greatly increased strain upon the others, thereby endangering the whole structure.*

4th. *Its parts are not of great weight or size, and may be easily transported, or put into or be taken out of place.*

5th. *It has a principle of renewal, allowing the easy displacement and replacement or interchange of any and all of its parts, without impairing or disturbing the material or workmanship of portions not needing renewal.*

6th. *Whether of large or small size, it has uniformly such elements of strength, as will always render it capable of sustaining many times greater pressure than need ever be demanded of it in practice, and its safety is not impaired by corrosion, or the many other harmful influences that so soon and so seriously affect the strength of ordinary boilers.*

7th. *Its parts are so made and put together that in case of rupture, no general break-up can occur. Its contents may be discharged, but no explosion or serious disturbance of any kind can take place, consequent upon such discharge.*

8th. *It is constructed so as to facilitate the removal of deposit of all kinds, from its interior and exterior surface.*

It is assumed that the better "guiding principles" in the construction of a steam-boiler have been fairly carried out,—that all other matters are at least equal, and that the result *is* a safer, if not a better one than any that has preceded it.

ITS PRACTICAL AND COMMERCIAL SUCCESS.

Until the spring of 1864, no effort was made to test the commercial merits of the Harrison Boiler by offering it for sale. In the early part of 1863 a boiler of fifty horse-power was put up experimentally at the establishment of Messrs. John Hetherington & Sons, Manchester, England, and subsequently a smaller one, at the same place. Both of these boilers worked well and gave great satisfaction up to the middle

ESSAY ON THE STEAM BOILER.

of 1864. Orders were also received for several others, to be erected in the neighborhood of Manchester. Several hundred tons of this boiler, made in England, were imported into this country in 1864, and put into operation in Philadelphia and other places.

Since October, 1865, I have been manufacturing the boiler at my own foundry on Gray's Ferry Road, Philadelphia. About fifty thousand horse-power of these boilers, varying from five to fifteen hundred horse-power, have been set at work since 1865, in various parts of the Union, from Maine to Texas, and from Massachusetts to San Francisco. Some have gone to Canada, others to South America, Liberia and New Zealand.

The advantages of the "Harrison Boiler" were understood and appreciated at the International Exhibition held in London in 1862, at which time a first-class medal was awarded to this invention, in Class VIII, *"for originality of design and general merit."*

The Harrison Boiler has met with more favor at the hands of the public than could have been expected, considering its material and the novelty of its form, and the prejudice that so naturally attaches to any effort aiming at an almost entire overthrow of a long established system. Its peculiarities invite criticism, and it would not appear strange if even many of those best acquainted with the subject generally, should pass this by with little attention, thinking at a glance that it was so much out of the beaten track, as to seem utterly impracticable.

Nothing in connection with the use of steam has been so much discussed, as the manner of making the apparatus for its generation, and to have called out, for a century past, such an army of thinkers on a subject having in the abstract but a few simple elements, there must have been, and no doubt still is, some inherent defect in the plans heretofore and now used.

If, in these pages, I have added to the stock of information tending to make the use of steam less dangerous to life and property, I have attained something. If I have been instrumental in producing a steam-boiler, that will take its place permanently, as a means of rendering steam-generating apparatus more safe from destructive explosion, I shall have attained something more. If in my effort to improve a much used and much abused object, manifestly demanding improvement, I have only succeeded in proving a fallacy, I shall still have my reward.

JOSEPH HARRISON, Jr.,
Rittenhouse Square, Philadelphia.

DIRECTIONS FOR USING

THE HARRISON STEAM BOILER.

IN screwing up the Harrison Boiler, the power of one man on a three-foot lever is all the strain that should ever be put upon the bolts. No amount of screwing will avail if the parts have been warped by overheating, or other cause. *The wrench should never be used while steam pressure is in the boiler.* Too low water is equally harmful to the Harrison Boiler as to all others, and should be most carefully avoided.

The Boiler should be blown out under full pressure, until empty, at least once a week, after the fire is drawn and the walls cooled below red heat. Especial care being taken that the bridge wall does not retain sufficient heat to warp the units during the interval of blowing off, which interval should be made as short as possible by refilling immediately.

When the Boiler is divided into two or more sections, or worked in connection with other boilers, then blow steam and water entirely out of one section under full pressure, retaining steam under full pressure in the other; and before closing blow-off cocks, turn full head of steam into the empty boiler. This rush of steam through all parts of the discharged boiler, if continued for a short time, will often drive out loose scale or soft matter, and do much to prevent injurious deposit.

In some instances, owing to the peculiar nature of the water, a soft or hard deposit will accumulate, and crack off, but not blow out as above. When this occurs it will be necessary to remove the lowest bolt in each slab for examination at least once in three months, and to clean out the deposit with a scraper. To do this the boiler room should be high enough to allow the bolt to be easily withdrawn.

Where water impregnated with lime is used in the Harrison Boiler it is advisable to use something to loosen the scale, as well as to prevent it

DIRECTIONS FOR USE. 35

from forming. In efforts to remove deposit, many of the patented anti-incrustation powders and liquids in vogue for this purpose have been tried, but nothing has been found better than *Crude Petroleum*. This may be poured in at the safety valve when steam is down, or forced in with the water by the pump. The quantity of oil to be used depends upon the character of the water.

It is not fair usage with the Harrison Boiler, or any other, to run it night and day, without intermission, for a week. Scale is thrown off from the inner surfaces by slight differences of temperature between the material of the boiler and the inside deposit of earthy or chemical matter, the latter being slightly broken by expanding or contracting less than the metal upon which it rests. To enable this difference of temperature to take place, it seems necessary that the boiler should be at rest, or nearly so, for a portion of the twenty-four hours of each day. Boilers running for six consecutive days of twenty-four hours each, and only cooled on the seventh day, may collect so thick a deposit that it will not scale or crack off with a single change of temperature. Under these circumstances any boiler should have the deposit removed by mechanical or other means, before it becomes so thick as to cause the material of the boiler to be unduly heated.

For the greatest efficiency in generating steam and economy in fuel, it is necessary that the external surface of the spheres should be kept at all times as clean as possible from ashes and soot. The best way to do this is by a steam-jet—an apparatus supplied with the Harrison Boiler. By using this jet for a few minutes, through the small doors in the fire front, once in twenty-four hours, exterior deposit can be easily removed.

When double sets of boilers are used of any kind—a single set being amply necessary for doing the work—then, unless in cases of emergency, such as repairs or cleaning, experience has shown, that economy in fuel, and durability in boiler and fittings, run entirely in the direction of working both sets of boilers all the time, or as near so as may be. Low fires induce low temperature in the chimney, a sure test of economy in fuel; and although the area of grate may be doubled, the saving will be surely found in the bills for coal. Working a boiler too hard, like overworking a good horse, tends to disablement. Boilers not used have a tendency to depreciate, just as horses are not benefited by standing idle too long in the stable.

REPORT*

OF THE

COMMITTEE ON SCIENCE AND THE ARTS,

CONSTITUTED BY THE FRANKLIN INSTITUTE,

ON THE

HARRISON STEAM-BOILER.

Invented by Joseph Harrison, Jr., Philadelphia, Pa.

THE Committee to whom was referred the examination of the "Harrison Boiler," report that, on Tuesday, October 30th, 1866, they visited the foundry of Mr. Joseph Harrison, Jr., Philadelphia, and had an opportunity of inspecting the boilers in various stages of manufacture, and of seeing several in operation.

Experiments were tried to prove the strength and durability of the boiler, under extraordinarily severe use.

These boilers are of cast iron, formed of a combination of hollow spheres, each eight inches diameter externally, and three-eighths of an inch thick, connected by curved necks three and one-quarter inches diameter. These spheres are held together by wrought iron bolts, and in one direction are cast in sets of two, or four, with opposite lateral openings to each sphere, and are called by the inventor two or four-ball units, as the case may be.

He assumes that the boiler, in its smallest form, may be considered as one of these balls, with its opposite lateral openings closed by caps held in place by bolts. Two balls united by a neck, with caps over the four lateral openings, in the same manner would also make a boiler of a larger size. Four balls so united in one casting, would be a still larger boiler, and that any number of these balls or spheres may be united by bolts passing through them so as to form large boilers, and

---

* See Journal of the Franklin Institute for February, 1867.

the strength of the boilers so made, will be the strength of the weakest sphere or ball in the structure.

In manufacturing the boiler for ordinary use, a number of these units are generally so arranged, as to form sections twelve and thirteen balls long, six balls wide, as shown by the annexed sketch A. These sections are all tested by hydrostatic pressure, as high as three hundred pounds per square inch, before being delivered to purchasers. The Committee saw one of these sections subjected to a bursting pressure of water, one sphere bursting when the pressure had reached six hundred pounds per square inch. A second one tested in the same manner, burst at six hundred and twenty-five pounds. They were shown a section in which one unit had burst at nine hundred pounds per square inch, the damage

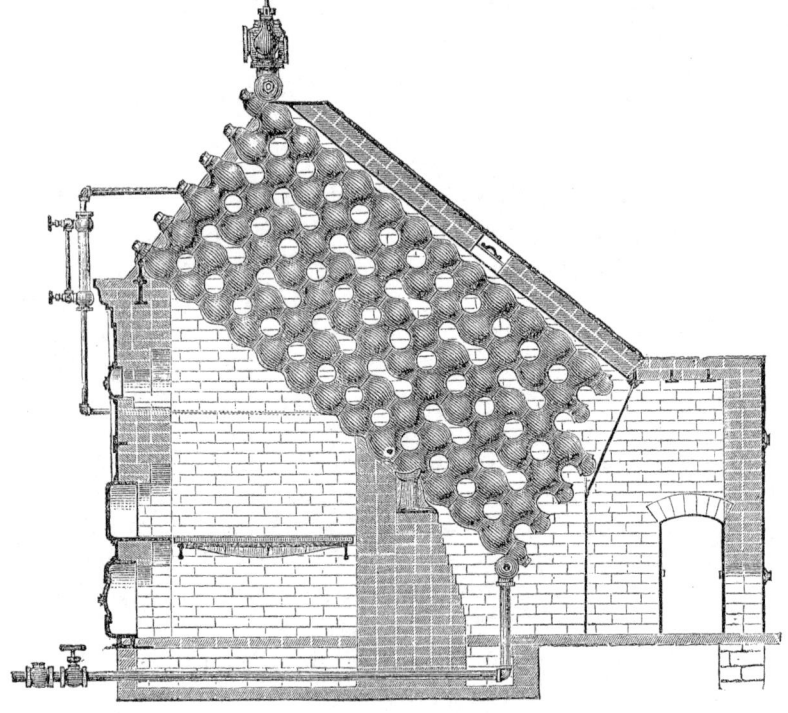

having been repaired by the insertion of a new unit. The section then stood eleven hundred pounds per square inch before bursting in a new place. The available strength of the section in all cases being the strength of the weakest unit in it, the inventor holds that the boiler is safer than any other in use; in fact, he considers it entirely free from any danger of disastrous explosion. To prove which, he had a section equal to six horse-power, similar to the one tested by hydrostatic pressure, and such as he is regularly selling, placed in an extemporary furnace built in a clay bank, and set in the usual manner for a boiler of this kind.

The boiler was filled with water to the regular height, say about two-thirds full, with no outlet or safety-valve of any kind, and sealed up tight, a small tube leading from the upper ball to a high pressure-gauge, placed at a safe distance, about two hundred feet, from the boiler. A fire was made under and around the boiler, with the fuel of dry pine wood. The wind was very high at the time of the experiment, blowing from the west directly into the furnace, thus fanning the flames to an intense heat.

The gauge soon gave indication of the formation of steam, the pressure steadily increasing up to four hundred and fifty pounds to the square inch.

At this pressure there seemed to be a sudden discharge of steam, as from a small opening. The discharge did not continue for many seconds, and the Committee are not certain that it proceeded from the boiler; there may have been some water discharged from the bank of wet earth into the fire. The pressure then increased at an uniform rate until it had reached the enormous strain of *eight hundred and seventy-five pounds per square inch*, when a sudden discharge of steam took place, seemingly no greater in volume than might issue from a safety-valve of two and a half inches diameter, or even less; after which the pressure fell to four hundred and fifty pounds, at which it stood when the fire was drawn for examination. While this boiler was being uncovered for examination, a boiler of about twelve horse-power, consisting of two sections, similar to the one previously experimented upon, was fired, and steam raised to one hundred and twenty-five pounds pressure. This boiler had no safety-valve, but was provided with a globe-valve of one inch capacity or area, as an escape-valve to regulate the pressure in the boiler. When the Committee examined this boiler at time of firing, it had two full gauges of water. The escape-valve was opened so as to reduce the pressure to one hundred pounds per square inch, and regulated from time to time to keep the pressure uniform at this point. The fire was pushed, and no more water injected into the boiler. In due time the lowest gauge-cock gave no indication of water. Soon afterwards a slight leak was observed in one joint of the left-hand section. This closed in a few minutes, and one opened in a similar manner in the right-hand section; this also closed in a short time. No other leaks showed themselves during the experiment. As the water boiled away, the soot began to burn off the upper balls of the sections, that is, off those of the upper balls of the lowest row, visible through a peep-door above the fire-door provided for inspection. The boiler then gradually became red-hot, and even when all the water seemed to be exhausted, and the pressure slowly fell, the gauge stood for some minutes at thirty pounds, as if from the vaporization of some water in the lower courses of the sections, showing that in this red-hot condition, the boiler was tight enough to hold pressure. After the fire had been drawn, and the boiler cooled, the bolts holding the units together were found to be loose, as if stretched by the unusual heating of the cast iron surrounding them. During the time of the experiment with low water, the escape-cock was many times closed to increase the pressure, then opened quickly to reduce it to the one hundred pound standard, but with no deleterious result. When the gauge stood at thirty pounds, all of the boiler visible from the peep-door and fire-doors, down to the bridge-wall of the furnace, was at a bright red heat. This was unmistakable, as, when the fire was drawn, the boiler was hot enough to ignite wood held against it.

November 13*th*, 1866.—At four o'clock, P. M., the Committee met at the factory. J. Agnew and J. C. Cresson present. They examined the boilers tested at the former meeting. The boiler which had been subjected to its own steam-pressure of eight hundred and seventy-five pounds per square inch, had been removed to the factory for examination. Mr. Harrison's foreman stated, that when the boiler was first dragged from the fire, after its water had been forced out, (as detailed in the account of the experiment,) the three lower bolts were quite slack, but the next morning, when it had become cold, one of them was again tight. The other two were not quite tight, but were then screwed up about one turn of the nuts. The Committee are confirmed in their belief that in this extreme test, the pressure at eight hundred and seventy-five pounds, was enough to stretch some of the bolts, that the joints opened as safety-valves, and thus relieved the strain on the boiler.

The boiler which, in former experiments, had had all its water boiled out, and had then been heated to bright redness, was found to be quite sound and fit for use, making steam freely, and showing no leak, blowing off at sixty-five pounds by the safety-valve. It was somewhat disfigured on its outside, by oxidation. Your Committe was informed that it had not been changed or repaired since the trial, but that some of the bolts had been screwed up.

A third boiler of the same size as the above, twelve horse-power, was then tested in the following manner: After being filled with water to the upper water-line, it was fired until pressure was raised to ninety pounds, at which it was blowing-off freely. The water was then all blown out by the blow-off cock, the pressure falling to sixty pounds while blowing-off, at which it stood until steam reached the blow-off pipe, when the pressure fell to zero. It was kept empty for three minutes, with the fire still burning, and was then rapidly filled with cold water, and steam raised to one hundred pounds pressure in thirty minutes, blowing off at one hundred pounds, and was quite sound and tight.

The Committee was informed by one of its members, who was a witness of, and cognizant of, all the facts, that at the establishment of Mr. Wm. Sellers & Co., of this city, a boiler of this kind has been in use for about two years. During some experiments in testing the Giffard Injectors made by that firm, a workman inadvertently loosened a connection to the water supply-pipe, resulting in the pipe blowing full open, discharging the water from the boiler as fast as a two-inch diameter opening would allow, the men in the boiler-room barely escaping with their lives. As soon as all the water had blown off, and access could be had to the boilers, the fires were drawn and cold water run in as fast as possible, and in about thirty minutes, the steam was high enough to run the engine, with no seeming injury to the boilers.

The Committee mention this as an accidental experiment, similar to the one above reported. The same boiler is still in use, and seemingly as good as when first erected. It is, however, the first one erected in this country from units made in England, and is not so good as those made since then. On Saturday, November 17th, Mr. Harrison repeated an experiment in the presence of a part of the Committee, Messrs. Agnew, Morton and Sellers, which experiment he stated had been tried twice the day before, and once two days previous, all the experiments being with the same boiler. The experiment, as witnessed, was as follows:

The boiler which had been under experiment November 13th was fired up, and steam raised to one hundred and ten pounds. The fire was active,—what might be called a very clear fire,—and in good condition to make steam freely. It had been kept up sufficiently long to thoroughly heat all the furnace walls. Steam was blowing-off freely from the safety-valve. At a given signal the blow-off cock was opened suddenly, blowing off all the water, until the pressure had fallen to zero, and neither steam nor water was escaping from the blow-off cock. In fact, it is believed the boiler was entirely dry. The blow-off cock was then closed, and cold water from a well pumped rapidly into the hot boiler, for it was at all times exposed to the active fire. As the water entered the boiler, the pressure as per gauge, rose slowly during an interval of about three minutes, when it is supposed the water-level had reached the more heated portion of the boiler above the bridge-wall of the furnace, for the pressure seemed instantly to increase to one hundred and ten pounds, and steam blew freely from the safety-valve.

This pressure and escape of steam, continued for some minutes with no variation, when suddenly an escape of steam was evident from the boiler into the furnace, and upon opening the peep-hole door a jet of water was seen issuing from one of the joints. This leak, in less than a minute, suddenly stopped; then, as the water rose in the boiler, a similar sudden leak and sudden stoppage, occurred at the next higher joint; again, at a third one, when, by that time, the water was showing itself at the lower gauge-cock, soon afterwards at the second one, when the pump was stopped, at which time the pressure stood at one hundred and ten pounds, steam blowing off freely from the safety-valve. The fire was as active as when the experiment began, and the boiler perfectly tight. This experiment, as before remarked, had been repeated three times previous to the one witnessed by the Committee, and Mr. Harrison's account of the previous experiments, given to your Committee, agreed in every respect with the facts as seen by them. This is as severe a test as any boiler is ever accidentally caused to sustain, and is, in fact, the one most likely to occur from carelessness. It is also testing practically, the favorite theory to account for explosions. During the experiments, the employees of Mr. Harrison seemed quite fearless in their manipulation of the boilers, showing a confidence in their safety, truly remarkable. With the exception of the single boiler sealed up and submitted to the extreme pressure of eight hundred and seventy-five pounds to the square inch, all the experiments were tried within the building in which the boilers are made, and any explosion would have resulted in serious loss of property, if not of life. Had any ordinary wrought iron boiler, made in the simplest form, and of the best material, been submitted to these same tests, it would have probably been destroyed by any one of them. Regarding the liability to accumulation of sedimentary deposit in this kind of boiler, we can only say that it is asserted by those who have used them the longest, that by occasionally blowing out the water under a full head of steam, then allowing the empty boiler to be moderately heated by the hot furnace, filling up with water and rinsing out, the scale becomes detached and rushes out at the blow-off cock.

The Committee have carefully inspected the manner of making these boilers as practiced by Mr. Harrison, and find the greatest care is taken to insure perfection of workmanship; but, at the same time, it is eminently noteworthy, that the peculiarities of the boiler, and its mode of manufacture, are such as to enable a high degree of mechanical excellence to be obtained by mechanical devices, apart from the workman's skill. Thus, in the process of casting, taking as an example a four-ball unit, the four eight-inch spheres united by necks three and a quarter inches diameter, internally, have on each ball two opposite lateral openings, three and a quarter inches diameter, thus making in all, eight openings to four balls. The patterns are all of cast iron, parted lengthwise through the centre of the unit, by a plane at right angles to the lateral openings, these serving as supports to the green sand core which is moulded within the pattern itself, and not in a separate core-box, thus insuring absolute uniformity to the thickness of the metal, and offering a more yielding core to the contracting metal than in the case of dry-sand moulding. The lateral necks which are to serve as joints in combining the units into the boiler structure, are faced off by machinery of the most ingenious kind, so arranged as to insure neat accuracy in the surface, the joints on one side having depressions to match projecting tongues on the other, these tongues serving with the longitudinal bolts to hold the units in position. One of the most thorough descriptions of this kind of boiler is the report of a paper read by Mr. Zera Colburn before the Institute of Mechanical Engineers in 1864, an abstract of which can be found in *Engineering Facts and Figures*, by A. Betts Brown, for 1864. He shows, that although the tensile strength of cast iron is not so great as wrought iron, yet the spherical form of each unit of the boiler gives it an equivalent strength. He says: "The strength of a hollow sphere to resist internal pressure, is exactly twice that of a hollow cylinder of the same diameter, material and thickness, and it can be shown that even a cast iron sphere, seven feet in diameter and seven-sixteenths of an inch thick, is as strong as the shell of a Cornish boiler of the same dimensions." "The plane in which rupture, if it happen at all, will take place in a hollow sphere, is the largest plane that can be drawn through it, and the metal resisting the strain tending to cause rupture, is the whole section of metal bounding the plane." " In a hollow cylinder, the area upon which the greatest pressure tending to cause rupture, will be exerted, is that represented by the product of the length into the ' diameter of the cylinder.' " The ends of such a cylinder, add nothing to the strength of the cylindrical part, in case of a rupture beginning at the cylindrical part.* The spherical form of each part of this boiler is one of its marked advantages, not only so far as strength is concerned, but as enabling a much larger amount of surface to be exposed to the fire than in any form of combined cylinder. To the spherical form with the curved necks, has been ascribed by the inventor the property, which this boiler is asserted as having to cast its scale when emptied of water, as there is no seeming abutment for the arch of the crystallized scale to spring from. The value of cast iron, so far as durability is concerned, has long been conceded. The purer the iron the more readily does it corrode, while the mixture of even a small amount of carbon increases its ability to resist corrosion. Wrought iron water-pipe under ground soon rusts out. Cast iron, even of the same thickness, remains good after many years' use; in fact, is considered practically to suffer no deterioration. Wrought iron in boilers decays internally—the most rapidly where moisture and air both operate, as in the upper side of mud-drums, while they are often eaten through from the outside by trifling leaks, and the constant trickle of water over the surface. Wrought iron boilers are, according to the experiments of Fairbairn and others, so much weakened by the process of riveting, &c,. as to suffer a deterioration of about forty per cent. The Harrison boiler is made of pieces of as uniform strength as possible, united in a systematic manner. The uniting the units or pieces into mass, does not diminish their strength. In case of accident to any part of the boiler, the damaged part may be removed, and instead of being repaired, as is done with wrought iron boilers, new parts may be substituted, just as bricks may be taken out, and new ones replaced in a building. The patching of a damaged wrought iron boiler makes it weaker. The renewal of any part of the Harrison boiler gives it its original strength.

The experiments heretofore described, have been conducted to de-

---

* The metal effectively resisting the rupture in the cylinder, being only the length of the cylinder. Thus, by comparison, Mr. Colburn arrives at his conclusion as to the relative strength of the two forms. (See *Engineering Facts and Figures*, 1864, pages 12 and 13.)

termine the safety and durability of the boiler under unusual and severe usage, or rather to determine whether any danger can result from submitting this kind of boiler to those circumstances which, in ordinary wrought iron boilers, are thought to result in explosions, or great injury to the boiler.

The Committee are impressed with the great utility of the boiler, as one *perfectly safe and free from all danger of explosion, even when carelessly used.* This recommendation alone, in a humanitarian point of view, must strongly commend it to public favor. During the experiments, its steam-making qualities were favorably noticed, and such boilers in actual use as your Committee have had an opportunity to examine, seem to give satisfaction in point of economy; but in the absence of all experiments in this direction, conducted under their immediate supervision, they do not feel qualified to report in figures as to its steam-making efficiency.

Comparing cast iron plates with wrought iron ones of the same thickness, the transmission of heat is known to be in favor of the former; hence the material, if in a safe form, is better adapted to economical steam-making, than wrought iron. Ordinary boiler plate is seldom less than one-fourth of an inch thick, and more commonly three-eighths, particularly for high pressure. The castings used in the experiments for safety, were not over three-eighths of an inch thick, and in one boiler set up in a form adapting it to marine purposes, some of the units were only three-sixteenths of an inch thick, and were worked successfully at one hundred pounds pressure, driving all the machinery in Mr. Harrison's factory in an efficient manner. The principle of enlargement of the boiler by addition of units, and the fact that it can be constructed in any shape or style, just as various kinds of buildings are constructed of ordinary bricks, places it in the power of the engineer to adapt it in its form to the requirements of each particular case; so that with the known advantage of the use of cast iron, and the unlimited scope in the arrangement of heat-absorbing surface, coupled with the demonstrated fact of safety, your Committee unhesitatingly *approve, and heartily recommend it to public favor.*

Sub-committee appointed to make the examination: Coleman Sellers, Chairman; John Agnew, John F. Frazer, Henry Morton, J. C. Cresson.

Note.—Notwithstanding the immunity in all respects with which these boilers withstood the unusual and most severe tests related above, still it is imperative that the proper height of water should be always maintained in the Harrison Boiler, as too low water is as likely to do injury to it as to any other.

LIFE-SAVING INVENTIONS.

LETTER FROM THE SECRETARY OF THE TREASURY,

IN ANSWER TO

A RESOLUTION OF THE HOUSE OF THE 15TH OF JANUARY, TRANSMITTING THE REPORT OF THE COMMISSION ON LIFE-SAVING INVENTIONS, CONVENED IN NEW YORK CITY, APRIL 8, 1867.

March 3, 1868.—Referred to the Committee on Commerce, and ordered to be printed.

TREASURY DEPARTMENT, March 2, 1868.

SIR:—I have the honor to transmit herewith, in compliance with House Resolution of the 15th of January, the Report of the Commission on Life-Saving Inventions, convened in New York, on the 8th of April, 1867.

Very respectfully, H. McCULLOCH,
Secretary of the Treasury.

HON. SCHUYLER COLFAX,
Speaker of the House of Representatives.

TREASURY DEPARTMENT, February 20, 1868.

SIR:—Pursuant to the instructions contained in your letter of the 3d of April last, I have the honor to report that I proceeded to the city of New York for the purpose of superintending the work of the Commission on Life-Saving Inventions, convened there, by your direction, on the 8th of that month.

The Commission was composed of Mr. A. S. Bemis, President of the Board of Supervising Inspectors; Messrs. John M. Weeks and John K. Matthews, of New York City, and Joseph Cragg, of Baltimore, local inspectors.

Here follows the Report, of which this is an extract of the portion referring to the Harrison Boiler:

THE HARRISON BOILER.

The peculiarity of this boiler renders a brief description of it necessary for those who may be unacquainted with it.

"It is constructed of hollow cast-iron spheres connected by hollow necks, all connected by means of bolts. Each casting is called a 'Unit.' Each 'Unit' has eight openings, their respective edges being faced fairly, so as to render the connection with the adjoining units complete. Each joint has a shoulder and socket, so as to secure the units in their places, and steam-tight caps to cover the outside openings. All the units, in whatever desired form they may be placed, are secured by adequate bolts passing through the spheres which contain the water and steam." This will suffice, with the aid of the cuts, to give an idea of this singular boiler. Cast-iron, applied to the ordinary form of boilers, was long ago discarded, but in the spherical form the strength is enormous, it never having been known to yield to a pressure less than 1,200 pounds to the square inch, and has even withstood a pressure of over 1,500 pounds. It is a portable, easily repaired, very durable, economical, and extremely safe boiler, and cannot be too strongly recommended.

It should be stated that, since the adjournment of the Commission, one of these boilers (a stationary one) has been continually under the notice of one of its most competent members, Mr. Cragg, of Baltimore, who speaks of it in terms of unqualified commendation—especially for land uses.

(Signed,) W. M. MEW.

Hon. H. McCULLOCH,
Secretary of the Treasury.

First Class Bronze Medal awarded to Joseph Harrison Jr., London, 1862. FULL SIZE. by the World's Fair. For originality of design and general merit.

First-Class Medal at the World's Fair, London,
1862.
"FOR ORIGINALITY OF DESIGN, AND GENERAL MERIT."

Only First Medal and Diploma at the American Institute Fair
NEW YORK, 1869.

At the American Institute Fair, the Harrison Boiler received the only First Medal and Diploma over all others. There were seven on Exhibition, besides an ordinary Firebox Tubular Boiler.

Two Harrison Boilers of fifty horse-power each, were exhibited, and as will be seen by the official report, were the only boilers put in operation on the ground, that were found reliable, and capable at all times of doing the work they were built to perform.

During the test of the Corliss Steam Engine, built by W. A. Harris, of Providence, R. I. these boilers, with feed water at a temperature of 47 degrees, furnished a horse-power for $3\frac{19}{100}$ pounds of coal per hour; developed seventy-six $\frac{57}{100}$ horse-power of boiler, being within $23\frac{43}{100}$ per cent. of their capacity. During part of the fair, they developed one hundred and twelve horse-power.

The principal competition was with two sixty horse-power Root Wrought Iron Sectional Boilers, advertised in the New York papers as of that capacity, and being sold to perform that amount of work. Owing to the priming of these boilers, and the leaking of steam and water, at the gum joints, at both ends of the tubes, they were found incapable, after repeated trials, of driving the larger engines, and were used to supply steam to the pumps on exhibition.

The Harrison Boilers were used for supplying steam to the engines, of which there were two of eighty, and three of fifty horse-power, requiring a large volume even without load.

Herewith, please find copy of the Official Report on Boilers and Certificates of Engineers, and Builders of Engines on Exhibition.

Report on Steam Boilers.

THIRTY-EIGHTH FAIR OF THE AMERICAN INSTITUTE HELD IN THE CITY OF NEW YORK, OCTOBER, 1869.

THE HARRISON SAFETY BOILER.—First medal and diploma for, 1st—Safety; 2d—Economy of Space; 3d—Economy of Fuel. This Boiler was the only one which was found reliable and capable of driving the engines at the Exhibition, and which did furnish all the steam for the competitive test of the engines.

ROOT'S WROUGHT IRON SECTIONAL BOILER.—Second medal and diploma for facility of repairs and economy of space.

A true copy from the report on file, adopted December 7th, 1869.

(Signed),

JNO. W. CHAMBERS, *Sec'y*.

Fair of American Institute.

NEW YORK, October 30th, 1869.

We, the undersigned, hereby certify, that the Two (2) Fifty (50) Horse-Power Harrison Safety Boilers have furnished the steam to the five Steam Engines on Exhibition, during the greater part of the past five weeks.

The Steam has been of good quality—abundant in quantity, and of uniform pressure.

The Boilers are tight, and have shown no leakage during the Exhibition—and their performance has been entirely satisfactory.

The Harrison Boilers were used during the present week in testing the Engines on trial.

WM. H. BUTLER, JR., Engineer Exhibition,
S. W. BLOOMER, " Rider Engine,
W. L. CRAIG, " Corliss,
T. D. BLAKE, of Geo. F. Blake & Co., Steam Pump Manuf'rs,
A. W. HARRIS, Harris Engine, (Corliss cut-off),
COLE BROS., Steam Fire Engine Builders,
PATRICK CLARKE, Patentee of Clark Blower,
JOHN COLLINS, Engineer,
W. A. HARRIS, Builder of Corliss Engine, Providence, R. I.,
WM. BAXTER, Patentee of Baxter's Portable Steam Engine,
GEO. C. CREAGER, in charge of Merrick & Son Steam Hammer,
C. M. VAN LINE, Loomis Engine.

First Class Bronze Medal awarded
Joseph Harrison Jr.
New York
1869
by the
American Institute Fair,
For the best Steam Boiler,

FULL SIZE.

Great Gold and Silver Rumford Medals awarded

Joseph Harrison, Jr.

Boston, Mass.

May 30th 1871.

FULL SIZE.

by the

American Academy of Arts and Science.

For his method of constructing Steam Boilers by which great safety has been secured.

[From the Philadelphia *Public Ledger*, January 12th, 1872.]

AWARD OF THE RUMFORD MEDALS, 1871

COUNT RUMFORD AND HIS USEFUL WORKS.

THE ORIGIN OF THE MEDALS, AND WHO HAVE RECEIVED THEM.

RUMFORD'S "MEDALS" AND WORKS.

"An Associated Press telegram, dated Boston, January 9th, announces that the "American Academy of Arts and Sciences" met that evening, for the purpose of presenting the "Rumford" medals to Joseph Harrison, Jr., of Philadelphia, for his "invention of safety boilers." The award of the medals was made at the last annual meeting of the Academy (1871), and the correspondence on the subject, together with a brief account of the origin of the fund, and of the previous awards of the medals, will be found in our news columns. Among the former recipients of the "Rumford medals" in America and in Europe, will be found the names of Dr. Robert Hare, of Philadelphia; John B. Ericsson and George H. Corliss, of our own country; and Sir Humphrey Davy, Michael Faraday, Sir David Brewster, F. J. D. Arago, Henry Fox Talbot, Dr. Arnott and John Tyndall, abroad. In the United States the medals are provided for by a fund, placed by Count Rumford in charge of the American Academy of Arts and Sciences, Boston, and in Europe by a similar fund placed in charge of the Royal Society, London.

This recent award in the United States recalls to mind the highly useful works of a remarkable man whose memory is chiefly identified with European countries—England, Bavaria and France—although he was an American by birth and grew to manhood on this side of the Atlantic. The man who subsequently became so famous as "Count Rumford," was a native of the little village of Woburn, near Boston, born in March, 1753. His name was Benjamin Thompson. Left an orphan in his infancy by the death of his father, he got the village-school education of those early days; was apprenticed (1766) to an importer of British goods in Salem, Mass., reading, studying, working at mechanical contrivances, dabbling in philosophy, and going to school and to lectures at intervals; married in his twentieth year; was appointed major in the Colonial forces; fell under suspicion as to his loyalty, at the outbreak of the Revolution; was threatened with mob violence, fled from his home (Concord), got within the British lines at Boston, and went to England in 1776. After that, his career was very eventful. He was appointed Under Secretary of State for the Colonies, possessing great influence over Lord George Germaine; came back to America (1781) as colonel of a regiment of cavalry in the British service; returned to England (1785); went soon after (still being a British officer,) to France, where he attracted the notice of the Elector of Bavaria by his fine appearance on horseback; was invited to Munich, having first been knighted in England; and in Munich he arose, in a few years, to be the confidential adviser of the sovereign, chief officer of the State, Commander-in-chief of the army, and Minister to England; having, in the meantime, established a military academy, military workshops to promote industry among the soldiers, improved the roads, established a noble park in Munich, abolished a deplorable state of mendicancy in the city by providing Industrial Homes for the Poor, and made many valuable improvements and discoveries in the application of science to the mechanic arts and domestic affairs. For all this he was made "Count Rumford." He returned to England in 1795, founded the "Royal Institution, which has given to the world the invaluable discoveries of Humphrey Davy, Michael Faraday, and John Tyndall; endowed the Royal Society and the American Academy with the funds for the

"Rumford medals;" went to Paris in 1803, continuing his philosophical investigations there until 1814, when he died, leaving the residue of his estate to Harvard University, Cambridge, Mass.

The career of which the foregoing is the barest skeleton of a sketch was as wondrous as a romance. But the most remarkable characteristic of the man, after the magnetic attraction of his manner, was the tenacity with which he held, and the energy with which he urged, his idea of bringing science to bear upon the practical affairs and employments of common life. Whenever he was engaged in his laboratory, experimenting upon the properties of heat and the developments of chemistry, he was always on the lookout for some way of utilizing his discoveries in the improvement of chimneys, fire-places, grates, stoves, ovens, lamps, furnaces for steam-engines, cooking utensils, &c.. He taught England how to avoid waste of fuel, how to construct chimneys that would not smoke, how to build fire-places, and how to erect kitchens for great hospitals; and he taught Bavaria how to make even the beggars self-supporting, and how to prevent the soldiers from being drones and demoralizers of society, by giving them incentives to be industrious in camp. Nothing was beneath his craving to improve everything, and he employed himself as readily in improving a kitchen "roaster" or a saw-horse for a woodsawyer, as in his inquiries into the abstract principles of heat, light and chemistry. His uppermost thought was to have science directed "to the improvement of arts and manufactures;" "the encouragement of industry;" the promotion of "the comforts and conveniences of life," especially among "the poorer and more numerous classes of society." This is the main thought in nearly all of his instructive essays; it was the basis of his idea in founding the "Royal Institution," into which *he* introduced Humphrey Davy, then an obscure young man; and it was his principal thought in establishing perpetual funds in America and Europe for the medals for *useful* inventions and discoveries which have given occasion for these remarks.

The "Royal Institution," which occupies an unpretending building in Albermarle street, London, is well worthy of the study of those of our countrymen who devote, or think of devoting, large sums of money for the endowment of colleges, libraries, &c., most of which money is usually spent in "stately piles of architecture," and too often stop there. The "Royal Institution" did not cost a fifth part of what has been wasted in buildings in many instances out of private endowments in this country; yet what a mark *that* "Institution" has made in the world in the "*increase* of useful knowledge." The great secret has been that, instead of spending its funds in buildings, it has been expended in developing the abilities, and in enabling such men as Davy and Faraday and Tyndall to devote their lives to *original research.*"

HONORS TO A PHILADELPHIAN.

BOSTON, January 9, 1872.

The Society of the American Academy of Arts and Sciences met to-night for the purpose of presenting the "Rumford" medal to Jos. Harrison, Jr., of Philadelphia, for his invention of safety boilers.

The following correspondence on the subject had passed previous to presentation:

CAMBRIDGE, December 12, 1871.

JOSEPH HARRISON, JR.,
Philadelphia:

DEAR SIR:—The American Academy of Arts and Sciences, at their last annual meeting, awarded you their Rumford medal, on the ground that the mode of constructing steam boilers invented and perfected by yourself, secures great safety in the use of high pressure steam, and is therefore an important improvement in the application of heat. As Chairman of the Rumford Committee of the Academy, it is my pleasure, as well as my duty, to communicate to you this fact, and to inform you that, in accordance with a vote of the

Academy, passed this evening, the medals will be formally presented to you by the President at the next stated meeting, on Tuesday, the 9th of January next. It would be highly satisfactory to the members of the Academy if you could be present at that meeting and receive the medals in person, but if this is not possible, I will act as your proxy, and transmit the medals to you as soon as the meeting is over. Will you kindly inform me whether we may expect you, and if it is not possible for you to come to Boston, through what channel and to what precise address you desire the medals to be sent. The award consists of a medal of gold, with a duplicate of silver, having a value of about four hundred dollars. I have the honor to be your obedient servant,

JOSIAH P. COOKE, JR.

To the President and Members of the
American Academy of Arts and Sciences.

MR. PRESIDENT AND GENTLEMEN:

In receiving the Rumford Medals which have been awarded to me in so flattering a manner by the American Academy of Arts and Sciences, I fear I cannot express in suitable terms my appreciation of this most distinguished honor. I can therefore only say that I do esteem this compliment very highly indeed, and I shall ever cherish these tokens with the greatest pride. To my mind, there is nothing within the limits of science, at the present time, that is of more importance than the "application of heat" to the safe generation of steam; and to have won an acknowledged distinction in such a field, and to have been deemed worthy of the reward that your honorable society has bestowed upon me, fully repays me for many years of anxious, and often of discouraging effort. In what I have done I claim but little merit, beyond having called attention, for the last twelve years, to the great importance of the question, and in having, in some degree, demonstrated the fact that a steam generator can be made secure from destructive explosion. I think that this idea has now taken such a firm hold upon the public mind, both in this country and in Europe, that it may be fairly inferred that, in the future, the use of steam under pressure, no matter what form the apparatus may eventually assume, will not be attended with the disastrous results that are recorded in the past. In expressing my regret at being unable to attend your meeting on January the 9th, so as to receive the medals in person, I most sincerely thank you, Mr. President and Members of the American Academy of Arts and Sciences, for this very high mark of your approbation.

JOSEPH HARRISON, JR.

PHILADELPHIA, January 6th, 1872.

The following gives an account of the origin of these medals, and the names of those to whom they have been awarded. The "Rumford Medal" of the American Academy, is provided for by an endowment fund or gift of $5000, in the United States funds, to the American Academy of Arts and Sciences, of Boston, made by Count Rumford, in 1796. By the conditions of this endowment, the interest of the fund is to be applied, "every second year," to the procurement of two medals, one of gold and one of silver, in value equal to the amount of two years' interest of the fund ($600), and those medals (or their equivalent in money,) are to be awarded to the author of the most important discovery or useful improvement in the application of heat and life which shall, in the opinion of the Academy, "tend most to promote the good of mankind." Although the fund was provided at that early day, no discovery or improvement of sufficient importance, in the opinion of the Academy, appeared until 1839, when the first award was made to Dr. Robert Hare, of Philadelphia, for his compound oxy-hydrogen blowpipe and improvements in galvanic apparatus. Since then, the awards of the medal have been as follows; 1862, John B. Ericsson, for his caloric engine; 1865, Professor Daniel Treadwell (Harvard College), for improvements in the management of heat; 1867, Alvan Clark, for improvement in lens of refracting telescope; 1870, George H. Corliss, Providence, R. I., for improvements in the steam engine; 1871, Joseph Harrison, Jr., Philadelphia, for "the mode of constructing steam boilers invented and perfected by" [Mr. Harrison,] which "secures great safety in the use of high pressure steam, and is, therefore, an important improvement in the application of heat."

The endowment for the "Rumford Medal," to be awarded under the auspices of the Royal Society of England, was established about the same time, being a gift, by Count Rumford, of one thousand pounds sterling, the interest of which was to be used in the same way, and for the same "useful improvements" as in the case of the American Fund. It is a little curious that the first award of the English Rumford Medal (1802,) was to Count Rumford himself, for discoveries in the application of heat. Among those awarded the English Medal, are Sir Humphrey Davy (1815), Sir David Brewster, (1818), Augustin Jean Fresnel (1824), Macedonio Melloni (1834), Henry Fox Talbot (1842), Michael Faraday (1846), F. J. D. Arago (1850), Dr. Neill Arnott (1854), John Tyndall (1864). These are all illustrious names.

IN THE MATTER OF THE

APPLICATION OF JOSEPH HARRISON, JR.,

FOR AN EXTENSION OF HIS

LETTERS-PATENT, DATED OCTOBER 4th, 1859,

FOR IMPROVED STEAM BOILER.

APPLICANT'S STATEMENT.

For a considerable period of time prior to making my above invention, I had devoted much attention and thought to the subject of steam boilers, with the object of devising some plan of construction upon which to produce a boiler effective and economical yet secure from harmful explosion. Finally I determined upon the plan which forms the subject-matter of my above-entitled patent, and which consists, essentially, of any desired number of small cast-iron hollow spheres connected by curved necks, series of these spheres fitting together with rebate joints, and being held together by means of wrought-iron rods or bolts with caps at the ends.

I proceeded as expeditiously as possible to test the practicability of the idea, by having erected and put in operation at the works of Messrs. William Sellers & Co., Philadelphia, a boiler of about 75-horse power. This boiler was successfully used for driving the workshops of Messrs. Sellers & Co., for several months, and appeared to settle the question of the possibility of using such a boiler, without disturbing its integrity by irregularity of expansion and contraction consequent upon the action of fire.

The experiment, however, was expensive, and went to show that much special machinery must be provided to allow of the manufacture of the boiler on a mercantile scale.

About this time I was obliged to visit Europe for the benefit of my health, and remained abroad for three or four years. During this time I had boilers in accordance with my invention made in England, and two (made in this country), imported into France and Belgium, in which countries I had taken out letters-patent. The boilers imported into Paris and Brussels were experimental, and for the purpose of complying with the laws regarding operation of patented inventions. Their manufacture and importation was a source of great expense to me, and I was compelled also to pay for shop room for working the boilers. Nothing further could be done in those countries, the prejudice against the invention being very great, while in France there was a law prohibiting the use of cast-iron for boilers.

The boiler made in London was successfully used in a manufactory of chemical goods in that city for several years, and I received for it, to the best of my recollection, knowledge, and belief, the sum of £100, which however, did not near cover the expense of making it.

I also had a boiler made in Manchester for the London International Exhibition of 1862, where a first-class medal was awarded to the boiler for "originality of design and general merit."

Shortly afterward I had two experimental boilers put up at the works of Messrs. John Hetherington & Sons, Manchester, which boilers worked well and satisfactorily up to the middle of the year 1864.

I also had machinery for manufacturing the boiler made at the works of the Messrs. Hetherington, at very heavy expense, special machinery for turning and fitting the joints of the cast-iron spheres being especially costly. With this machinery a foundry was stocked at Openshaw, near Manchester, and preparations made for starting the manufacture of the boiler on a mercantile scale. Orders had been received for several boilers to be erected in the neighborhood of Manchester; but shortly after commencing this enterprise, my special agent in charge of it was disabled by sickness, and I sent another agent for the purpose of closing out the business.

I have no clear and reliable account of the expenses and receipts attending my proceedings abroad, excepting as regards the cost of the special machinery made, as I have above stated, in Manchester. This machinery, together with stock, scrap-iron, &c., in the foundry at Openshaw, was transferred to the factory which, in the year 1864, not long after my return to this country, I started at Gray's Ferry, this city, and figures in my account hereto annexed.

I am prepared to state, however, that my foreign patents, so far from being a source of revenue, were, in fact, a heavy loss to me.

Since the year 1864, I have been engaged continuously in the manufacture of my patented boiler in this city, and have succeeded, in the face of much prejudice and interested opposition, in creating a steady demand for it.

Up to this time (1873) boilers to the amount of about 50,000 horse-power have been sold and put in use, with results amply proving, as I expect to show by competent and disinterested testimony, the great utility and value of the invention.

Notwithstanding the extent, however, to which the invention has been introduced, it has on the whole been so far a source of heavy loss to me, and this from a variety of causes.

The invention was of a radical character—a wide departure from preconceived notions and settled custom. This fact, in addition to the strenuous opposition and slowness of belief which it naturally evoked, involved very great expense of time, labor, and money, in the provision of special means and modes of manufacture, the conducting of experiments, the drawing of public attention, and the trial of various real or supposed improvements in the details of manufacture with a view to increased efficiency and economy.

In view of the evident public importance of that principle of safety in boiler construction, which my invention was designed to introduce, and convinced of the correctness of the theory upon which that invention is founded, I have spared no time, labor, or expense in the endeavor so to construct the boilers that they should recommend themselves to boiler users, not only by reason of their safety, but also for general efficiency and economy. To this end I have tried from time to time various experiments in the details of manufacture and arrangement, without, however, departing from the patented features of the invention. Of these experiments some succeeded, and others were failures, involving great expense. As an example of this, I may cite a change, which in the year 1871, I temporarily adopted in the "set" of the boiler, with a view to increase its steam room. A number of boilers were sold and set up upon this changed plan, but it was found that the changed "set" caused the heat to interfere with the integrity of the structure. These boilers, therefore, I had to take back, and replace with others.

The "set" which has been found perfectly reliable is that illustrated on page 38 of the pamphlet hereto annexed, and marked Exhibit A.

The boiler has been submitted to many experimental tests of its safety and reliability, and has successfully withstood such trials as no wrought-iron boiler would endure.

In 1869, at the 38th fair of the American Institute, held in New York, the first medal and diploma was awarded to the Harrison Boiler for safety, economy of space, and economy of fuel, the boiler being the only one, according to the report, which was found reliable, and capable of driving the engines at the Exhibition, and which did furnish all the steam for the competitive tests of the engines.

*In 1871, the American Academy of Arts and Sciences, at Boston, awarded to me the Rumford medals, on the ground that my mode of constructing steam boilers secures great safety in the use of high pres-

---

* To show the significance and value of this reward to Mr. Harrison, it may be stated that but seven of these medals have been bestowed since the time when this committee was appointed by Count Rumford, at the beginning of this century. The gold medal is more than one pound in weight.

re steam, and, therefore, is an important improvement in the appli-
tion of heat.

UTILITY AND VALUE OF THE INVENTION.

These lie in a number of points, which may be enumerated as
llows:

1. *Safety.*—It appears absolutely impossible that there should be
y destructive explosion of the boiler. In the case of rupture, the
ints of the units become so many safety-valves to empty the contents
the boiler gradually.

2. *Economy.*—In first cost the boilers are cheaper than wrought-
on boilers of equal capacity of approved make, this advantage being
eater in respect to boilers of larger size. To the best of my infor-
ation, knowledge, and belief, as between a boiler of my make, hav-
g a thousand feet of heating surface, and a wrought-iron tubular
oiler of like surface, the average advantage of my boiler in the matter
first cost is not less than 15 per cent. It is a very important point,
so, in this question of economy, that owing to the facility with which
e material of which my boilers are made, may be re-used in the
anufacture, I am enabled to remove an old shell and replace it with
new one at half the cost of a first new boiler.

3. *Strength and Durability.*—Pressures and ill-usage, which no
dinary boiler could withstand, have been applied in my boilers
ithout materially affecting their integrity. In October and Novem-
er, 1866, a committee of the Franklin Institute overlooked several
xperiments made in my place to test these points, and their report
ill be found in the Journal of the Franklin Institute for February,
867, and a reprint thereof on pages 37 to 45 of the annexed pam-
hlet, Exhibit A.

4. *Ease of Transportation*, owing to the lightness and smallness
f the parts.

5. *Facility of Repair.*—Any or all parts of the boiler may be
splaced, replaced, or interchanged without impairing or disturbing
e material or workmanship of portions not needing repair. Units

of the boiler made to-day may be used for the repair of any of the boilers made within the last nine years.

6. *The material, cast-iron,* is not nearly so susceptible to the action of corrosion as is wrought-iron. It has been found in practice that my boiler may be used for a length of time without deterioration, in situations where previously wrought-iron boilers had been very rapidly destroyed by the corrosive action of the water used.

7. The boiler is of such construction as greatly to facilitate the removal of deposit either from the exterior or interior surface.

In the matter of the Application of Joseph Harrison, Jr., for an Extension of his Letters-Patent, No. 25,640, *dated October* 4th, 1859, *for "Improvement in the Construction of Steam Boilers."*

ATLANTIC CITY,
ATLANTIC COUNTY, } *ss.*
NEW JERSEY.

Joseph Harrison, Jr., the above named applicant, being duly sworn, deposes as follows:

In addition to what is said in my statement in regard to the utility and value of this invention, I desire to say that in the one respect of first cost alone, I believe that the total sales of my boilers, as set forth in my said statement, represent a saving to the public of not less than two hundred thousand dollars over the cost of wrought-iron boilers of equal aggregate capacity and approved construction. To this may be added the fact, proven by experience, that the average annual expense of repairs to the Harrison boiler is less than one per cent. of the original cost of the boiler, an economical condition which, to the best of my knowledge, information, and belief, cannot be approached by any other boiler in the market. Furthermore, I believe that the Harrison boiler is more durable than wrought-iron boilers of approved construction; but if we assume equal average durability, say ten to twelve years, this being the period allowed as the average life of a good wrought-iron boiler, to replace wrought-iron boilers originally costing one million three hundred thousand dollars would require renewed expenditure to at least the same amount; but I can replace my boilers at one-half the original cost, owing to the availability of the material, thus effecting a saving of over six hundred thousand dollars. This refers to the mere boiler itself. If, in addition, we take into account the costs of removal and re-setting, there is a great and very apparent saving resulting from the "divisibility" of my boiler. This is a very obvious advantage in the numerous cases where boilers are erected in the cellars of buildings or other confined and inaccessible situations.

Again, taking the item of cost of transportation, all the parts of boilers of my construction can be moved to great distances at fourth class or the lowest rates of freight, while wrought-iron boilers, requiring to be moved bodily, can be transported only at special high rates. It is evidently impossible to find with any degree of accuracy the "ascertained value" of my invention. The figures which I have hereinbefore given, amounting to over eight hundred thousand dollars, constitute, I believe, a reasonable estimate of that ascertained value in respect to the two items of first cost, and cost of renewal. What may have been the aggregate savings in respect to the items of economy in repairs, in consumption of fuel, in cleaning, in transportation, in the occupancy of space, I cannot pretend to state, but believe them to have been very great. But the chief value of my invention, the end for which it was designed, is safety to persons and property. Its value in this respect cannot of course be figured. Suffice it to say that there has not been one case of "destructive explosion" in the use of boilers of my construction.

JOSEPH HARRISON, Jr.

Sworn and subscribed before me this ninth day of September, A. D. 1873. As witness my hand and the certificate seal of Atlantic City, N. J.

JOHN J. GARDNER,
Mayor of said city.

In the matter of the application of Joseph Harrison, Jr., for an Extension of his Letters-Patent, No. 25,640, dated October 4th, 1859, for "Improvement in the Construction of Steam Boilers."

CITY AND COUNTY OF PHILADELPHIA, } ss.
STATE OF PENNSYLVANIA.

Daniel Allen, being duly sworn, deposes:

I am   years of age; reside in this city; and am a dyer by occupation. I am conversant with the patented boiler manufactured by the above named applicant, and consisting of a series of cast-iron spheres with finished joints, and united by wrought-iron tie-rods, having had such boilers in use in my establishment for about six years last past. At the present time I have in use two of said boilers of fifty horse-power each. Of these boilers, one consists of sections which I procured from the ruins of a *sugar-house in this city, which was burned down about two years ago. These sections had been subjected for a considerable time to a heat sufficiently intense to melt the brass connections of the boilers. They had been on the ground floor of one of the very largest sugar refineries in the city, and which the fire had tumbled into a mass of ruins. These sections—spheres and bolts—upon test were found perfectly sound, and I have ever since been using the fifty horse-power boiler which was built up from them without repair, saving the replacing of one of the spheres by another at a cost not exceeding five dollars.

I have found the Harrison boiler more economical in the matter of the consumption of fuel than any others I have used during the experience of eighteen or nineteen years.

I have used ordinary cylinder boilers and locomotive boilers. In my opinion the Harrison boiler is, as compared with the cylinder boiler, from one-third to one-fourth more economical in the con-

---

* Newhall, Borie & Co., Crown and Race Streets.

sumption of ordinary fuel for a given amount of duty, while it is fully as economical in that respect as the locomotive boiler, or even more economical. In one feature of economy I have found the Harrison boiler to possess an advantage which I have not found in either of the other kinds of boilers I have named, *i. e.*, in the possibility of consuming the waste of the factory, such as spent dyewood, as fuel.

To do this an extent of grate surface is required, which I have found it impracticable to obtain with the cylinder or locomotive boiler, but which the "set" peculiar to the Harrison boiler secures.

Another advantage which I have found the Harrison boiler to possess, and which gives it especial value in my business, is in the dryness of the steam which it gives off In this regard I consider the boiler infinitely superior to any other of which I have knowledge.

For these reasons, and on account of the perfect freedom of the boiler from liability to destructive explosion, I regard it as an invention of great value and importance to the public.

I have no interest in this application.

DANIEL ALLEN.

In the matter of the application of Joseph Harrison, Jr., for an Extension of his Letters-Patent No. 25,640, dated October 4th, 1859, for an "Improvement in the Construction of Steam Boilers."

CITY OF BOSTON,
COUNTY OF SUFFOLK, } *ss.*
STATE OF MASSACHUSETTS.

Gustavus A. Jasper, being duly sworn, deposes:

I am   years of age, and for seven years was superintendent of the Union Sugar Refinery in this city. I am conversant with the

Harrison boiler, consisting of a series of cast-iron spheres connected by finished joints, and united by wrought-iron tie-rods, six of said boilers, of fifty horse-power each, having been in use at the Union Refinery. On comparing the performance of the Harrison boiler with that of the wrought-iron tubular and flue boilers which we had previously used, it was found that four of the Harrison boilers would give all the steam wanted at a regular pressure, a result we could never attain with the six old boilers, and a very close and accurate account of the consumption of fuel from December, 1867, to December, 1868, showed a very great saving over the old boilers, and this during a period when we refined a greater quantity of sugar than ever before.

Since September, 1870, I have been connected and interested with the Standard Sugar Refinery of Boston, and at the present time have in use in said refinery seven hundred horse-power of Harrison boilers, all of which give great satisfaction. I believe the Harrison boiler to be more economical in the consumption of fuel and respect to maintenance in good running order, than any other boiler of which I know. It is cheaply and readily repaired, above all, practically safe.

I do not hesitate to express my opinion that the Harrison boiler is an invention of the greatest public value and importance.

I have no interest in this application.

GUSTAVUS A. JASPER.

Sworn and subscribed to before me this fifth day of September, 1873.

SUMNER FLOYD,
Justice of the Peace.
14 Old State House, Boston.

In the matter of the Application of Joseph Harrison, Jr., for an Extension of his Letters-Patent No. 25,640, dated October 4th, 1859, for an "Improvement in the Construction of Steam Boilers."

SOUTH MANCHESTER,
HARTFORD COUNTY, } *ss.*
STATE OF CONNECTICUT.

SEPTEMBER 5th, 1873.

Rush Cheney, being duly sworn, deposes:

I am   years of age, and am a member of the firm of Cheney Brothers, silk goods manufacturers.

I am conversant with the above-entitled invention, fifteen Harrison boilers, making altogether ten hundred and fifty horse-power, being used by our firm, the first of said boilers having been put in about the year 1866. We have found the said boilers the best we know of for generating steam, and the most economical in fuel for the quantity of steam furnished. We had previously used both flue and tubular boilers.

We have also found the said Harrison boilers to be durable and of easy maintenance in good order, in constant use.

For these reasons, and for their undoubted safety, I consider the Harrison boiler to be an invention of great public utility and value.

I have no interest whatever in this application.

RUSH CHENEY.

Sworn and subscribed to this fifth day of September, 1873, before me,

CHARLES S. CHENEY,
Justice of the Peace.

In the matter of the Application of Joseph Harrison, Jr., for an Extension of his Letters-Patent No. 25,640, *dated October* 4th, 1859, *for an "Improvement in the Construction of Steam Boilers."*

CITY AND COUNTY OF PHILADELPHIA, } ss.
STATE OF PENNSYLVANIA.

George Wood, being duly affirmed, deposes:

I am   years of age; am President of the Millville Manufacturing Company, of Millville, New Jersey, manufacturers of cotton goods, and a member of the firm of R. D. Wood & Sons and of R. D. Wood & Co., of Philadelphia.

I have read the above-entitled letters-patent, and am conversant with the invention therein described and claimed.

The Millville Manufacturing Company has for about eight years past been using the boilers made by applicant, under his said patent, and consisting of a series of cast-iron spheres connected by finished joints and united by wrought-iron tie-rods.

The said company has in use at the present time such boilers to the amount of two hundred horse-power, and the said firm of R. D. Wood & Co. is also using like boilers to the amount of one hundred horse-power.

My experience is that the Harrison boiler compares favorably with wrought-iron tubular or flue boilers of good construction and equal capacity in the matters of economy of fuel, efficient performance of duty, and durability. As regards readiness and cheapness of repairs, I know of no boiler that will compare with the Harrison boiler, the advantage of which in these respects is attributable partly to the peculiarity of construction, and partly to the nature of the material (cast-iron) of which the shell of the boiler is composed. A burnt-out wrought-iron shell is of no value, save as scrap, while the material of a worn-out Harrison boiler is readily available in the manufacture, and therefore of great relative value.

I consider that the Harrison boiler is perfectly free from liability to destructive explosion, and on this point I can speak from personal experience.

On one or two occasions the Harrison boilers used by our company have by accident suffered treatment such as in my opinion would, in the case of wrought-iron boilers, have been likely to result in destructive explosion. In each case the effect upon the Harrison boiler was simply to cause leakage at the joints, which thus acted as so many safety-valves.

For the foregoing reasons I consider the applicant's invention to be one of the greatest utility, value, and importance to the public.

I have no interest in this application.

GEORGE WOOD.

Affirmed and subscribed before me, this twenty-ninth day of August, A. D. 1873.

WM. A. STEEL,
Notary Public.

In the matter of the Application of Joseph Harrison, Jr., for an Extension of his Letters-Patent No. 25,640, dated October 4th, 1859, for an "Improvement in the Construction of Steam Boilers."

ANSONIA, NEW HAVEN COUNTY, } ss.
STATE OF CONNECTICUT.

William Wallace, being duly sworn, deposes as follows:

I am   years of age, and am a member of the firm of Wallace & Sons, manufacturers of brass goods. I am conversant with the above-entitled invention. Wallace & Sons have had the Harrison boiler in use for over five (5) years, and employing at the present time about one hundred and seventy-horse-power. In the course of business I have paid much attention to the subject of steam generators, with the object of finding the best and most economical generator for our work.

With the Harrison boiler careful experiments were conducted for weeks in our establishment, for the purpose of determining the relative value of the boiler in comparison with others we had in use. On comparison with a first-class tubular boiler of equal capacity it was found that with one pound of coal the Harrison boiler evaporated $11\frac{29}{100}$ pounds of water as against $8\frac{88}{100}$ pounds evaporated in the tubular boiler; and the experiment continued for ten hours showed a saving in favor of the Harrison boiler of 575 pounds of coal for a like quantity of water evaporated.

It was found also that the steam generated by the Harrison boiler was much drier. In addition to this economy the Harrison boiler, while in my opinion it is at least as durable as a first-class wrought-iron boiler, is much more readily and cheaply repaired than any other boiler known.

We have also found that the material (cast-iron) of the shell of the boiler is not so susceptible to corrosion as wrought-iron, and that the construction of the boiler greatly facilitates the removal of deposit either from the interior or exterior surface.

For these reasons, and still more on account of its unquestionable "safety," I consider the Harrison boiler an invention of the greatest value and importance to the public.

I have no interest in this application.

WILLIAM WALLACE.

Sworn and subscribed before me, this second day of September, 1873.

S. A. COTTER.

REPORT OF EXAMINER.

Hon. M. D. Leggett,
Commissioner of Patents.

Sir :—In the matter of the Application of Joseph Harrison, Jr., for the Extension of the Patent granted him October 4th, 1859, No. 25,640, for Improvement in Steam Boilers. I have the honor to make the following report:

The Invention.—The invention consists in making the boilers numerous spheroidal sections, made singly or in groups, connected by joints and held together by stay-bolts. The object of this construction of boilers is to secure the greater relative strength of the sphere over any other form containing the same quantity of metal; the increased heating surface and the facility with which the boiler may be transported, erected and repaired.

Claims.—The claims are as follows :—The construction of a boiler of distinct globular or spherical parts, singly or in groups substantially as above described, united in the manner hereinbefore specified or any other analogous thereto, and wherein the strength of the globular form of such parts is common to the entire structure.

This claim being intended to include not true spheres only, but elliptical, conical, polyhedral, or any other analogous forms also, when the results looking to strength and construction of the boiler are substantially the same as those herein enumerated.

I also claim the employment as units of construction, as hereinbefore explained, of separate chambers of cast-iron or other metal, of uniform size and shape, substantially as described to be used as wanted, where with boilers of different forms and dimensions may be built up, being united together in the manner hereinbefore specified, or any other analogous thereto.

These claims, although not such as would be allowed in an application at the present day fully cover the invention and are unambiguous, and therefore open to no serious objections.

State of the Art.—Prior to this invention several boilers had been made involving the principles of its construction, and accomplishing in a manner the object to be attained by it.

See page 12 to page 17 inclusive of Hancock's Common Road Steam Carriages published 1838, in which a boiler composed of sections is described, each chamber or section being provided with hemispherical projections from each side, said chambers all communicating and held together by stay-bolts. This boiler, however, can only be enlarged longitudinally by placing more chambers side by side and using longer bolts.

In the English patent, No. 111, 1856, small retort boilers are variously disposed in the furnace and properly connected. The capacity of the boiler may be increased by adding new chambers. Boilers are constructed "so that the various parts may readily be replaced or substituted one for another when improved and be easy of transportation, with large amount of heating surface."

In the English patent, No. 2047, 1857, small bottle-shaped chambers are connected by pipes to a common steam receiver, each section being separately heated by gas.

It is evident, however, that applicant's invention was considerably in advance of the art of constructing boilers of this class as shown by the above at the date of his patent.

Value and Importance to the Public.—The importance to the public is shown by the testimony of several competent persons.

Remuneration.—Applicant's own statement as to his efforts to introduce his invention are full and satisfactory. The invention was first introduced at the works of Messrs. William Sellers & Co., of

Philadelphia, where a boiler of seventy-five horse-power was erected and gave satisfactory results.

At this period applicant was compelled to go to Europe for his health.

He appears to have made good use of his time by introducing his invention in England, Belgium and France, and secured patents in said countries. At Manchester several boilers were made and put in use where also a manufactory was established. The agent in charge became disabled by sickness, wherefore applicant sent another agent for the purpose of closing out the business.

Since 1864 applicant has been continuously engaged in manufacturing his boiler in the City of Philadelphia, and up to the present time boilers to the amount of fifty thousand horse-power have been sold and put in use.

Applicant's foreign patents and his efforts to introduce his invention in Europe, as also his experiments and efforts in this country have been a heavy loss to him.

No testimony has been filed to support applicant's statement as to his efforts to introduce his invention, or to show that his failure to receive a proper remuneration was not caused by fault or neglect on his part. His statement of receipts and expenditures, and the fact that several parties have made oath that they have used his boiler would necessarily imply that he has used due diligence, and in fact has made constant endeavors to reap a reward for his invention. No attempt is made to give an ascertained value. The value as applicant states being primarily in the prevention of destructive explosions, the value and importance of which cannot be expressed in dollars and cents.

Receipts and Expenditures.—The account is not made particular and in detail, but the aggregate receipts and expenditures for each year is given; which, however, is sufficient to enable the office to come to a correct conclusion as to applicant's remuneration.

Applicant states that he has no data in his possession which enable him to give an account of receipts and expenditures in connection with his foreign operations, he asserts moreover that they were attended by considerable loss.

This may explain why his account begins with the year 1864 instead of the date of his patent.

In conclusion it may be said that the invention was new at the time patented—that it is of great value and importance to the public—that the applicant has not been sufficiently remunerated for his time, ingenuity and expense, and that such failure was not caused by negligence or fault on his part.

Respectfully submitted,

M. B. PHILLIPP,
Examiner.

SEPTEMBER 16th, 1873.

REPORT OF EXAMINERS IN CHIEF.

UNITED STATES PATENT OFFICE,
SEPTEMBER 27th, 1873.

Application of Joseph Harrison, Jr., for the Extension of the Patent for Steam Boilers, granted to him October 4th, 1859.

TO THE HON. COMMISSIONER OF PATENTS.

We respectfully submit the following report:

The examiner in charge has made a thorough investigation into the novelty of the invention, and there is no reason for questioning his conclusions in its favor.

The evidence as to its value and importance is very full, and justifies placing upon it a high estimate. The original cost of the boilers is from one quarter to one third less than those constructed in the ordinary way. When past further use the materials can be employed in the fabrication of new boilers by which a large saving is effected. They are not so liable to have scale form in them, and when formed it is easily removed without taking off with it any of the metal. For this and other reasons they endure longer and cost less in repairs. They produce more steam in proportion to the fuel burned in them, and it is drier. There have been manufactured what would amount to fifty thousand horse-power. From these data which he specifies more particularly, the applicant seems to be well warranted in estimating the value of the invention at $800,000.00. Its chief merit, after all, consists in the immunity it affords from explosions with their attendant danger to life and property, a merit which it would be hard to appreciate.

Ill health drove the applicant to Europe soon after obtaining his patent, and he obtained patents in England, France and Belgium. He labored with energy to introduce his invention in those countries without any success in the latter two. He established works for producing his boiler in England at a heavy expense. But after his return to this country the agent to whom the management of his business abroad was entrusted, became unable from sickness to conduct it, and he was consequently compelled to relinquish all these undertakings, and to bring home the furniture of his English works. In these foreign operations he incurred a loss. The expenses attendant upon his endeavors to establish works in this country, and to introduce his boiler, have been very energetic and extensive, and have entailed upon him a further loss, over and above all his receipts.

There cannot an objection be raised against the extension of his patent, and he has earned it well.

In the matter of the Application of Joseph Harrison, Jr., for an Extension of his Letters-Patent, dated October 4th, 1859, for Improved Steam Boiler.

CITY AND COUNTY OF PHILADELPHIA, }
STATE OF PENNSYLVANIA. } *ss.*

Thomas L. Luders, being duly sworn according to law, deposes:

I am   years of age, and have been acquainted with the above named applicant for about twenty years last past. I have read the statements of said applicant as to his efforts to introduce the invention, both in this country and in England, France and Belgium, and believe the same to be correct. I was personally connected with said efforts from the time of the erection of the first of said patented boilers at the works of William Sellers & Co., in the City of Philadelphia, until the year 1864. I know that after the erection of said boiler, Mr. Harrison was for a time prevented by sickness from giving personal attention to any business, and that he resided in Europe for several years for the benefit of his health. I know that during his said residence in Europe, applicant used his best endeavors to introduce the invention into use in England, France and Belgium, employing me to assist him as his agent to that end, and expending very large sums of money for the purpose. The work done in England as set forth in applicant's statement was under my personal supervision. I know that applicant's endeavors to introduce the invention in these countries were met with hostile prejudice, and that his foreign patents so far from being a source of any profit to him caused him very large expense.

This was owing to various causes, the opposition above referred to, and the great expense of time, money, and labor required to prepare the necessary machinery and tools for manufacturing the boiler on a commercial scale, and with that nicety of accuracy which is requisite. To illustrate this I may state that when under applicant's instruction I was preparing one of the patented boilers for the World's Fair at London in 1862; to prepare the joints of the spheres cost one English shilling per joint, whereas, at the present time said work costs not more than one cent per joint. This difference has been attained by special elaborate machinery, the costly character of which may be deduced from the fact that each of the first two machines made for the purpose weighed seven and a-half tons.

The fact is that it required the experience of the several years labor given to the invention in England to prepare for the manufacture of the boiler on a commercial scale, and that it was the experience and material thus acquired at great expense which enabled applicant in the year 1864 to commence the manufacture of a boiler in this city in a large way.

Since January, 1872, I have been engaged in Applicant's Boiler Works as "Superintendent," and prior to that time I had intimate personal relations. I can, therefore, speak from knowledge of applicant's assiduous efforts to popularize his boiler. I know that he has expended large sums of money in advertisements, in the publication of elaborate circulars, and in public and private tests of the boilers, for the purpose of illustrating its safety and economy, and that he has employed agents in different parts of the Union for the introduction of the boiler. I know, too, that he has not hesitated to devote much time and labor and large sums of money to the object of reducing the details of manufacture to the most perfect and economical system. It is within my knowledge too that applicant has all along had to face and overcome much prejudiced and interested opposition.

I do not doubt that it is entirely owing to applicant's persistency and unstinted devotion of his private means to the work of introducing the invention, that its present firm establishment as a recognized manufacture is due.

For the reasons above given, I state without hesitation my belief that applicant's failure to derive proper remuneration from his invention has been through no fault of his.

I have also read applicant's supplemental statement as to the ascertained value of the invention, and believe the estimate there given to be a reasonable one, as to the value in the two only points in which that value can be estimated.

I have no interest in this application.

THOMAS L. LUDERS.

Sworn and subscribed this twenty-third day of September, A. D. 1873.

WILLIAM A. STEEL,
Notary Public.

In the matter of the Application of Joseph Harrison, Jr., for an Extension of his Letters-Patent No. 25,640, dated October 4th, 1873, for an "Improvement in the Construction of Steam Boilers."

CITY AND COUNTY OF PHILADELPHIA, }
STATE OF PENNSYLVANIA. } ss.

Samuel Harrison being duly sworn, according to law, deposes:

That he is   years of age; that from the year 1864, to December, 1871, he was engaged as consulting engineer by applicant, at his Boiler Works, at Gray's Ferry, in the City of Philadelphia. Deponent can speak from knowledge of applicant's industrious efforts, and liberal expenditure of money during that period of time, to popularize his said patented boiler, and to improve and extend the manufacture thereof. The invention was a radical change in the art of boiler making, and required for its manufacture special new machinery and appliances. The boiler works at Gray's Ferry were started with machinery and stock which, as deponent is informed and believes, had been made for applicant in England, and which were of a very expensive character. After the starting of the works applicant was unsparing in his labor and expenditure to add to and improve the machinery and tools, in order to facilitate and economize the manufacture. Furthermore, he tried, during the time deponent was with him, many and costly experiments to test and demonstrate the capabilities of the boiler, to determine the most advantageous "set," in a word, to furnish to the public a boiler which should recommend itself, not only on account of its safety, but by reason of its economy and general utility.

In his efforts applicant had to contend with much hostile prejudice and interested opposition, in addition to the difficulties naturally attending the development and public introduction of an invention so radically novel.

Defendant had also knowledge of the endeavors of applicant to draw the attention of the public to the invention, and to introduce it by advertisement, by circulars, and by the appointment of agents in different cities of the Union.

Deponent believes that the present firm establishment of the manufacture is owing to applicant's persistent diligence and unstinted expenditure of his private means, and that his failure to derive sufficient remuneration from his patent has been without fault on his own part.

Deponent is no relation of applicant, is not now, and has not been for eighteen months last past connected with him in business, and has no interest whatever in this application.

SAMUEL HARRISON,
No. 108 Tulpehocken Street, Germantown, Philadelphia.

Sworn to and subscribed this twenty-fourth day of September, A. D. 1873.

WILLIAM A. STEEL,
Notary Public.

ARGUMENT.

In the matter of the application of JOSEPH HARRISON, JR., *for an extension of his Letters-Patent, No.* 25,640, *October* 4th, 1859, *for "Improvements in the construction of Steam Boilers."*

TO THE HON. COMMISSIONER OF PATENTS.

Sir:—The records of extension cases do not present many instances like the present, of wealth, and years of persistent industry, voluntarily devoted to the attainment of an object of great public utility.

It may be stated here, as a matter of general notoriety, that applicant is one of those American engineers who, in the early history of railroad construction in Russia, illustrated the reputation of their nationality for mechanical ingenuity and skill.

The means and personal repute thus earned removed from applicant the ordinary incentives to diligence and enterprise. But applicant's activity would not permit him to lead the life of ease to which he might have been thought to be entitled; he must be occupied; and his occupation was not the further accumulation, which would have been so easy, but an unstinted expenditure of thought, time, labor and money, to the development and practical realization of an idea which he justly regarded as calculated greatly to benefit the public.

Applicant's statement and the testimony, show that the work, which he thus voluntarily imposed upon himself, was one of no ordinary magnitude. It involved the facing and overcoming of the accepted traditions of years of theorizing, and of practice in the art to which the invention belongs.

Applicant could not hope that the undeniable safety of his boiler would alone recommend it to public favor, unless he could demonstrate that the boiler would sustain a comparison with those ordinarily used in respect to cost, general efficiency, and economy in use.

This was a matter of time—no isolated experiments, however satisfactory in their results to the projector, would serve to convince an unbelieving public.

Owing to the lack of machinery and tools adapted to the peculiar work, the first boilers made here and abroad, involved expense which must be very greatly reduced before commercial competition with other boilers could be thought of. Costly machinery and tools therefore had to be provided while the enterprise was still in an experimental stage, with few believers other than the applicant himself. When the facilities for manufacturing the boiler on a mercantile scale were provided, the work of educating the public to a belief in it could be fairly begun. So far the result to applicant, during a period of five years of the term of the patent, had been continuous loss, nor could he, even now, look forward to speedy remuneration.

His account shows an excess of expenditure over receipts for seven of the nine years, during which the boiler has been manufactured here on a commercial scale. This is owing to the extraordinary efforts which applicant has made to build up and sustain a trade in the face of much opposition to perfect the manufacture.

We cannot do better here than quote his own statement.

"In view of the evident public importance of that principle of safety in boiler constructions which my invention was designed to introduce, and convinced of the correctness of the theory upon which the invention is founded, I have spared no time, labor, or expense in the endeavor so to construct the boilers, that they should recommend themselves to boiler users, not only by reason of their safety, but also for general efficiency and economy. To this end I have tried from time to time various experiments in the details of manufacture and arrangement without, however, departing from the patented features of the Invention."

In this testimony applicant is fully confirmed by the testimony of Thomas L. Luders and Samuel Harrison. They tell us that applicant so far from being disposed to let well enough alone, was constant in his endeavors and unsparing in his expenditure in experiments and tests to demonstrate or to increase the capabilities of the boiler.

Nor while thus diligent to develop the merits of his invention, was applicant neglectful of proper means to make the patent remunerative. Clyde testifies to the expenditure of no less than fifty thousand dollars in advertising. That applicant's enterprise has been on the whole a loss to himself is evidently owing to no want of energy or business tact on his part, but simply because of the great difficulties to be surmounted, and because he has subordinated the question of private profit to the important public end he aimed at—that of producing a boiler at once safe and efficient.

PRIOR STATE OF THE ART.

In his report the Examiner refers to the "Hancock" boiler as being composed of communicating sections, held together by stay bolts. But apart from the fact pointed out by the Examiner that this boiler can only be enlarged longitudinally by placing more chambers side by side and using longer bolts, and thus lacks the essentials of economy of space, ease of erection, and repair and general availability, it is evident that it further differs from applicant's boiler in that its sections are not "units of strength and safety."

It is evident that any explosion of a Hancock boiler would probably be as disastrous in its results as the explosion of any wrought iron boiler.

The Examiner also refers to English Patent No. 111 of 1856, and No. 2047 of 1857, but neither of these appears to merit serious consideration in the case.

As the Examiner remarks, it is evident that applicant's invention was considerably in advance of the art of constructing boilers of this class, as shown by the above at the date of his patent.

It may be admitted that applicant was not the first to propose a sectional boiler, but he undoubtedly was the first to construct a boiler in which perfect safety should be united with, and conduce to, portability and ease of construction and repair.

REMUNERATION.

The Examiner reports that applicant's own statements as to his efforts to introduce his invention are full and satisfactory, but objects to the want of testimony in support of it. To remove this objection the affidavits of Thomas L. Luders and Samuel Harrison have been filed, which fully confirm applicant's statement. Mr. Luders testifies to the work done by applicant abroad, and Mr. Harrison to his efforts in this country, and both express their belief, formed on personal knowledge, that applicant's failure to derive sufficient remuneration from his patent has been from no fault of his own. The facts that the applicant has established and continued at great cost works for the manufacture of the boilers, and has made and sold them to the extent of fifty thousand horse-power, would certainly seem to be sufficient proof of reasonable diligence, but it is apparent from the testimony that he has exercised such diligence as few men would or could have exercised, and that it is to the self-sacrificing character of his diligence that this failure to derive adequate remuneration is largely due.

ASCERTAINED VALUE.

The Examiner further reports that no attempt is made to give an ascertained value—a somewhat erroneous statement. In his supplemental affidavit of September 9th, 1873, applicant has given an estimate of the ascertained value, so far as regards the items of first cost and costs of repairs, based upon the number of boilers actually made and sold. The figures thus arrived at show an ascertained value of more than eight hundred thousand dollars in the two respects named, and this estimate the witness, Luders, regards as reasonable. Were this *all* the value, it would warrant the grant of the extension asked for. But as applicant justly remarks, it is evidently impossible to find with any degree of accuracy the "ascertained value" of the invention. Its primary value is in safety to persons and property. "There has not been one case of destructive explosion in the use of the boiler," and all the witnesses testify to the value of the invention in this respect. But it is an element of value which cannot be reduced to figures.

Then there are the incidental advantages of the divisibility and consequent portability and ease of construction and repair of the boiler, its economy in the occupancy of space, &c., all manifestly important items, yet incapable of definite computation.

ACCOUNT.

The Examiner objects to this, that the account is not made sufficiently particular and detailed, but gives the aggregate receipts and expenditures for each year. This objection, however, is qualified by this statement, that the account is sufficient to enable the office to come to a correct conclusion as to applicant's remuneration.

By the affidavit of James Clyde, it appears that the account is a transcript carefully made from the books of the establishment. The original copy made under the personal supervision of the witness is attached to his affidavit, and is somewhat more in detail than that furnished by applicant, owing to the separation of the expense account into "Purchases" and "Expenses," the witness explaining that under the former head are included the cost of machinery, tools, material and fuel, and under the latter salaries of employés, commissions to agents, advertising, experiments, and the various minor details which are legitimately included in the expense account of any mercantile business.

Witness also gives reasons for the non-inclusion in the first account of items for the first half of the present year, and the statement of his affidavit and the accounts annexed thereto are further verified by the affidavit of applicant.

It is respectfully contended that the figures presented comply with the requirements of the law, in constituting an account sufficiently full and in detail fairly to show the profit and loss arising from the patent.

The fact upon which the Examiner comments, that the account begins with the year 1864, is fully accounted for. That was the year in which the manufacture was started here, and systematic book accounts commenced. Before that there had been very heavy expenses abroad, but of these there are no reliable data, the invention however is debited in the account rendered with the cost valuation of making and importing the machinery, tools and materials collected in England.

We cannot doubt that your Honor will concur in the Examiner's conclusion that the invention was new when patented, is of great value and importance to the public, and that without negligence or fault on his own part, applicant has not been adequately remunerated for the time, ingenuity, and expense devoted to the invention.

Very Respectfully Yours,

HOWSON & SON,
Attorneys for J. Harrison, Jr.

PHILADELPHIA, September 26, 1873.

CERTIFICATE OF EXTENSION.

WHEREAS, upon the petition of Joseph Harrison, Jr., of Philadelphia, Pennsylvania, for the Extension of the Patent granted to him October 4, 1859, for an "IMPROVED STEAM BOILER;" the undersigned, in accordance with the Act of Congress, approved the 8th day of July, 1870, entitled "An Act to revise, consolidate, and amend the statutes relating to patents and copyrights:" did, on this third day of October, 1873, decide that said Patent ought to be extended.

Now, THEREFORE, I, Mortimer D. Leggett, Commissioner of Patents, by virtue of the power vested in me by said Act of Congress, do renew and extend the said Patent, and certify that the same is hereby extended, for the term of seven years from and after the expiration of the first term, viz.: from the fourth day of October, 1873, which certificate being duly entered of record in the Patent Office, the said Patent has now the same effect in law as though the same had been originally granted for the term of twenty-one years.

And it is hereby ordered that this certificate of extension be entered on a certified copy of said Patent.

In testimony whereof, I have caused the seal of the Patent Office to be hereunto affixed, this third day of October, 1873, and of the Independence of the United States the ninety-eighth.

M. D. LEGGETT,
Commissioner.

Printed in Dunstable, United Kingdom